RELIGIONS
OF THE
WORLD

BUDDHISM

CHRISTIANITY

CONFUCIANISM

HINDUISM

ISLAM

JUDAISM

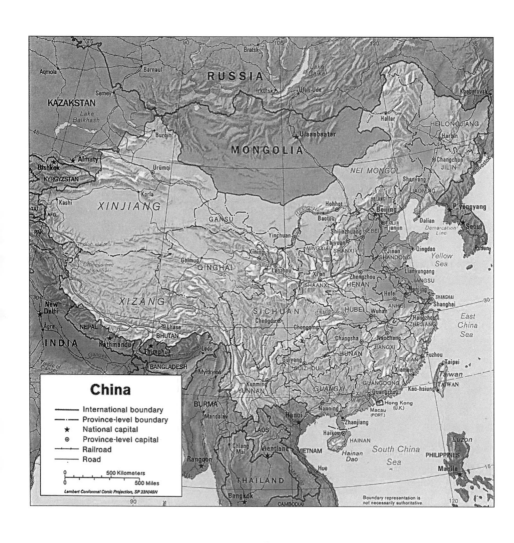

China

International boundary
Province-level boundary
★ National capital
⊙ Province-level capital
Railroad
Road

0   500 Kilometers
0   500 Miles
Lambert Conformal Conic Projection, SP 23N/46N

RELIGIONS
OF THE
WORLD

CONFUCIANISM

Rodney L. Taylor
Professor of Religious Studies,
University of Colorado, Boulder

Series Consulting Editor Ann Marie B. Bahr
Professor of Religious Studies,
South Dakota State University

Foreword by Martin E. Marty
Professor Emeritus,
University of Chicago Divinity School

CHELSEA HOUSE
PUBLISHERS
A Haights Cross Communications Company
Philadelphia

DEDICATION
For Megan, Annika, and Dylan, my children:
May they further the next generation of learning

FRONTIS   This map shows some of the places in which Confucianism had
its strongest influence, including China, Taiwan, and Vietnam.

CHELSEA HOUSE PUBLISHERS

VP, NEW PRODUCT DEVELOPMENT   Sally Cheney
DIRECTOR OF PRODUCTION   Kim Shinners
CREATIVE MANAGER   Takeshi Takahashi
MANUFACTURING MANAGER   Diann Grasse

Staff for CONFUCIANISM

EXECUTIVE EDITOR   Lee Marcott
SENIOR EDITOR   Tara Koellhoffer
PRODUCTION EDITOR   Megan Emery
ASSISTANT PHOTO EDITOR   Noelle Nardone
SERIES AND COVER DESIGNER   Keith Trego
LAYOUT   21st Century Publishing and Communications, Inc.

www.chelseahouse.com

First Printing

9 8 7 6 5 4 3 2 1

Library of Congress Cataloging-in-Publication Data

Taylor, Rodney Leon, 1944–
    Confucianism : Rodney L. Taylor.
       p. cm.—(Religions of the world)
Includes index.
    ISBN 0-7910-7857-4 HC   0-7910-8010-2 PB
    1. Confucianism. I. Title. II. Series.
BL1852.T38 2003
299.5'12—dc22
                                            2003023920

CONTENTS

Foreword

On this very day, like all other days, hundreds of millions of people around the world will turn to religion for various purposes.

On the one hand, there are purposes that believers in any or all faiths, as well as unbelievers, might regard as positive and benign. People turn to religion or, better, to their own particular faith, for the experience of healing and to inspire acts of peacemaking. They want to make sense of a world that can all too easily overwhelm them because it so often seems to be meaningless and even absurd. Religion then provides them with beauty, inspires their souls, and impels them to engage in acts of justice and mercy.

To be informed citizens of our world, readers have good reason to learn about these features of religions that mean so much to so many. Those who study the faiths do not have to agree with any of them and could not agree with all of them, different as they are. But they need basic knowledge of religions to understand other people and to work out strategies for living with them.

On the other hand—and religions always have an "other hand"—believers in any of the faiths, and even unbelievers who are against all of them, will find their fellow humans turning to their religions for purposes that seem to contradict all those positive features. Just as religious people can heal and be healed, they can also kill or be killed in the name of faith. So it has been through history.

This killing can be literal: Most armed conflicts and much terrorism today are inspired by the stories, commands, and promises that come along with various faiths. People can and do read and act upon scriptures that can breed prejudice and that lead them to reject other beliefs and believers. Or the killing can be figurative, which means that faiths can be deadening to the spirit. In the name of faith, many people are repressed, oppressed, sometimes victimized and abused.

If religion can be dangerous and if it may then come with "Handle with Care" labels, people who care for their own security, who want to lessen tensions and inspire concord, have to equip themselves by learning something about the scriptures and stories of their own and other faiths. And if they simply want to take delight in human varieties and imaginings, they will find plenty to please them in lively and reliable accounts of faiths.

A glance at television or at newspapers and magazines on almost any day will reveal stories that display one or both sides of religion. However, these stories usually have to share space with so many competing accounts, for example, of sports and entertainment or business and science, that writers and broadcasters can rarely provide background while writing headlines. Without such background, it is hard to make informed judgments.

The series RELIGIONS OF THE WORLD is designed to provide not only background but also rich illustrative material about the foreground, presenting the many features of faiths that are close at hand. Whoever reads all six volumes will find that these religions have some elements in common. Overall, one can deduce that their followers take certain things with ultimate seriousness: human dignity, devotion to the sacred, the impulse to live a moral life. Yet few people are inspired by religions in general. They draw strength from what they hold particularly. These particulars of each faith are not always contradictory to those of others, but they are different in important ways. It is simply a fact that believers are informed and inspired by stories told in separate and special ways.

A picture might make all this vivid: Reading about a religion, visiting a place of worship, or coming into the company of those who believe in and belong to a particular faith, is like entering a room. Religions are, in a sense, spiritual "furnished apartments." Their adherents have placed certain pictures on the wall and moved in with their own kind of furnishings, having developed their special ways of receiving or blocking out light from such places. Some of their figurative apartments are airy, and some stress strength and security.

Philosopher George Santayana once wrote that, just as we do not speak language, we speak particular languages, so we have religion not as a whole but as religions "in particular." The power of each living and healthy religion, he added, consists in "its special and surprising message and in the bias which that revelation gives to life." Each creates "another world to live in."

The volumes in this series are introductions to several spiritual furnished apartments, guides to the special and surprising messages of these large and complex communities of faith, or religions. These are not presented as a set of items in a cafeteria line down which samplers walk, tasting this, rejecting that, and moving on. They are not bids for window-shoppers or shoppers of any sort, though it may be that a person without faith might be drawn to one or another expression of the religions here described. The real intention of the series is to educate.

Education could be dull and drab. Picture a boring professor standing in front of a class and droning on about distant realities. The authors in this series, however, were chosen because they can bring readers up close to faiths and, sometimes better, to people of faith; not to religion but to people who are religious in particular ways.

As one walks the streets of a great metropolis, it is not easy and may not even be possible to deduce what are the faith-commitments of those one passes unless they wear a particular costume, some garb or symbol prescribed by their faith. There-fore, while passing them by, it is not likely that one can learn much about the dreams and hopes, the fears and intentions, of those around them.

These books, in effect, stop the procession of passersby and bid visitors to enter those sanctuaries where communities worship. Each book could serve as a guide to worship. Several years ago, a book called *How to Be a Perfect Stranger* offered brief counsel on how to feel and to be at home among worshipers from other traditions. This series recognizes that we are not strangers to each other only in sanctuaries. We carry over our attachments to conflicting faiths where we go to work or vote or serve in the military or have fun. These "carryovers" tend to come from the basic stories and messages of the several faiths.

The publishers have taken great pains to assign their work to authors of a particular sort. Had these been anti-religious or anti–the religion about which they write, they would have done a disservice. They would, in effect, have been blocking the figurative doors to the faiths or smashing the furniture in the sanctuaries. On the other hand, it would be wearying and distorting had the assignment gone to public relations agents, advertisers who felt called to claim "We're Number One!" concerning the faith about which they write.

Fair-mindedness and accuracy are the two main marks of these authors. In rather short compass, they reach a wide range of subjects, focusing on everything one needs to advance basic understanding. Their books are like mini-encyclopedias, full of information. They introduce the holidays that draw some neighbors to be absent from work or school for a day or a season. They include galleries of notable figures in each faith-community.

Since most religions in the course of history develop different ways in the many diverse places where they thrive, or because they attract intelligent, strong-willed leaders and writers, they come up with different emphases. They divide and split off into numberless smaller groups: Protestant and Catholic and Orthodox Christians, Shiite and Sunni Muslims, Orthodox and Reform Jews, and many kinds of Buddhists and Hindus. The writers in this series do justice to these variations, providing a kind of map without which one will get lost in the effort to understand.

Some years ago, a rabbi friend, Samuel Sandmel, wrote a book about his faith called *The Enjoyment of Scriptures*. What an astonishing concept, some might think: After all, religious scriptures deal with desperately urgent, life-and-death-and-eternity issues. They have to be grim and those who read them likewise. Not so. Sandmel knew what the authors of this series also know and impart: that the journeys of faith and the encounter with the religions of others include pleasing and challenging surprises. I picture many a reader coming across something on these pages that at first looks obscure or forbidding, but then, after a slightly longer look, makes sense and inspires an "aha!" There are many occasions for "aha-ing!" in these books. One can also wager that many a reader will come away from the encounters thinking, "I never knew that!" or "I never thought of that before." And they will be more ready than they had been to meet strangers of other faiths in a world that so many faiths *have* to share, or that they *get* to share.

Martin E. Marty, Professor Emeritus
The University of Chicago

Preface

The majority of people, both in the United States and around the world, consider religion to be an important part of their lives. Beyond its significance in individual lives, religion also plays an important role in war and peace, politics, social policy, ethics, and cultural expression. Yet few people feel well-prepared to carry on a conversation about religion with friends, colleagues, or their congressional delegation. The amount of knowledge people have about their own faith varies, but very few can lay claim to a solid understanding of a religion other than their own. As the world is drawn closer together by modern communications, and the religions of the world jostle each other in religiously plural societies, the lack of our ability to dialogue about this aspect of our lives results in intercultural conflict rather than cooperation. It means that individuals of different religious persuasions will either fight about their faiths or avoid the topic of religion altogether. Neither of these responses aids in the building of healthy, religiously plural societies. This gap in our knowledge is therefore significant, and grows increasingly more significant as religion plays a larger role in national and international politics.

The authors and editors of this series are dedicated to the task of helping to prepare present and future decision-makers to deal with religious pluralism in a healthy way. The objective scholarship found in these volumes will blunt the persuasive power of popular misinformation. The time is short, however. Even now, nations are dividing along religious lines, and "neutral" states as well as partisan religious organizations are precariously, if not always intentionally, tipping delicate balances of power in favor of one religious group or another with doles of aid and support for certain policies or political leaders. Intervention in the affairs of other nations is always a risky business, but doing it without understanding of the religious sensitivities of the populace dramatically increases the chances that even well-intentioned intervention will be perceived as political coercion or cultural invasion. With such signs of ignorance already manifest, the day of reckoning for educational policies that ignore the study of the world's religions cannot be far off.

This series is designed to bring religious studies scholarship to the leaders of today and tomorrow. It aims to answer the questions that students, educators, policymakers, parents, and citizens might have about the new religious milieu in which we find ourselves. For example, a person hearing about a religion that is foreign to him or her might want answers to questions like these:

- How many people believe in this religion? What is its geographic distribution? When, where, and how did it originate?

- What are its beliefs and teachings? How do believers worship or otherwise practice their faith?

- What are the primary means of social reinforcement? How do believers educate their youth? What are their most important communal celebrations?

- What are the cultural expressions of this religion? Has it inspired certain styles of art, architecture, literature, or music? Conversely, does it avoid art, literature, or music for religious reasons? Is it associated with elements of popular culture?

- How do the people who belong to this religion remember the past? What have been the most significant moments in their history?

- What are the most salient features of this religion today? What is likely to be its future?

We have attempted to provide as broad coverage as possible of the various religious forces currently shaping the planet. Judaism, Christianity, Islam, Hinduism, Buddhism, Confucianism, Taoism, Sikhism, and Shinto have each been allocated an entire volume. In recognition of the fact that many smaller ancient and new traditions also exercise global influence, we present coverage of some of these in two additional volumes titled "Tribal Religions" and "New Religions." Each volume in the series discusses demographics and geography, founder or foundational period, scriptures, worldview, worship or practice, growing up in the religion, cultural expressions, calendar and holidays, history, and the religion in the world today.

The books in this series are written by scholars. Their approach to their subject matter is neutral and objective. They are not trying to convert readers to the religion they are describing. Most scholars, however, value the religion they have chosen to study, so you can expect the general tone of these books to be appreciative rather than critical.

Religious studies scholars are experts in their field, but they are not critics in the same sense in which one might be an art, film, or literary critic. Religious studies scholars feel obligated to describe a tradition faithfully and accurately, and to interpret it in a way that will allow nonbelievers as well as believers to grasp its essential structure, but they do not feel compelled to pass judgment on it. Their goal is to increase knowledge and understanding.

Academic writing has a reputation for being dry and uninspiring. If so, religious studies scholarship is an exception. Scholars of religion have the happy task of describing the words and deeds of some of the world's most amazing people: founders, prophets, sages, saints, martyrs, and bodhisattvas.

The power of religion moves us. Today, as in centuries past, people thrill to the ethical vision of Confucianism, or the dancing beauty of Hinduism's images of the divine. They are challenged by the one, holy God of the Jews, and comforted by the saving promise of Christianity. They are inspired by the stark purity of

Islam, by the resilience of tribal religions, by the energy and innovation of the new religions. The religions have retained such a strong hold on so many people's lives over such a long period of time largely because they are unforgettable.

Religious ideas, institutions, and professions are among the oldest in humanity's history. They have outlasted the world's great empires. Their authority and influence have endured far beyond that of Earth's greatest philosophers, military leaders, social engineers, or politicians. It is this that makes them so attractive to those who seek power and influence, whether such people intend to use their power and influence for good or evil. Unfortunately, in the hands of the wrong person, religious ideas might as easily be responsible for the destruction of the world as for its salvation. All that stands between us and that outcome is the knowledge of the general populace. In this as in any other field, people must be able to critically assess what they are being told.

The authors and editors of this series hope that all who seek to wield the tremendous powers of religion will do so with unselfish and noble intent. Knowing how unlikely it is that that will always be the case, we seek to provide the basic knowledge necessary to critically assess the degree to which contemporary religious claims are congruent with the history, scriptures, and genius of the traditions they are supposed to represent.

Ann Marie Bo Bahr
South Dakota State University

1

Introduction

Man is a living thing; the Buddhists speak not of life
but of death. Human affairs are all visible. . . .

—Hu Yin (1098–1156)

The Confucian tradition has played a major role in the lives of countless people across all of East Asia and parts of Southeast Asia for over two thousand years. From humble beginnings within a small circle of people, Confucianism has grown to be closely associated with virtually every aspect of the countries that have practiced it, whether political, cultural, or societal. To speak of Confucianism is to speak of the ideology of national and state governments as well as the education of private individuals. Confucianism has influenced the educational system at national, regional, and local levels, including the tutoring of kings and commoners alike. It also impacts literature and the arts, norms of behavior, and all segments of society, both men and women, from the highest class of educated elite to the great majority of ordinary people. The Confucian influence has stretched across the broad sweep of history from its founding to the contemporary age. Today, it is even discussed in Western circles because of its global impact on the diversity of cultures and their worldviews.

SIZE AND DISTRIBUTION

It is no exaggeration to say that all of East Asia—that is, China (both mainland China and Taiwan), Korea, and Japan—along with parts of Southeast Asia (particularly Singapore and Vietnam), as well as overseas Asian communities, are part of the sphere of influence of the Confucian tradition. This distribution suggests a worldwide tradition that plays an important role in the lives of its adherents regardless of whether they are living in an Asian culture or elsewhere, such as in the United States or Europe. However, Confucianism has, throughout almost all of its history, been associated mainly with people of Asian origins. Although there has been some recent movement toward Confucianism among non-Asians as the religion is discussed more often in the West, whether it will have any long-lasting influence is as yet difficult to assess.

Given the very wide distribution of Confucianism historically and culturally, one might ask just how many people are Confucians. The question is an important one because its answer illustrates something very central about Asian religious traditions in general and about Confucianism specifically. Often in the discussion of various religious traditions, an estimate will be given of the approximate number of adherents, or members, of a particular religion. There are, for example, so many million Jews, Christians, or Muslims in the United States or worldwide. In each of these cases, it is presumed that when someone is identified as a member of one of these religions, he or she is not at the same time part of another religion. In other words, a person is not both Jewish and Christian or both Christian and Muslim. Each religion is largely exclusive of other religions.

In the sphere of influence of Confucianism, however, exclusive membership is not a requirement. For example, in plotting the distribution of Chinese religions, China has often been called the culture of three religious traditions—Confucianism, Taoism, and Buddhism. Popular religions, including faiths focused upon local deities and spirits that are not part of the major traditions, might be added to this. In Korea, people mainly practice traditional local religion, Confucianism, Buddhism, and, in recent times, Christianity. Japan is principally Shinto, Confucian, and Buddhist, with a few cults that fall outside of these major classifications. It is difficult, if not impossible, to say that a certain percentage of the population in East Asia is Confucian as opposed to either Taoist or Buddhist. This is because many individuals in that culture hold a religious worldview or engage in practices that may come from all three Asian religious traditions. Being part of all three traditions is not viewed as a conflict. Confucianism is an inclusive, not exclusive, approach to religion. This inclusiveness is a hallmark of Asian culture in general.

What, then, is the overall number of adherents of Confucianism? The answer lies in understanding that Confucianism has been fundamental to the people of East and Southeast Asia through-out their history. In many respects, almost all Asian people are in some fashion influenced by the Confucian tradition, and the people often live in ways that reflect these ideas and practices, but not exclusively.

IS CONFUCIANISM A RELIGION?

To ask whether Confucianism is a religion might seem like a very strange question, but it points to one of the unique features of the Confucian tradition. After all, would anyone ask whether Judaism, Christianity, Islam, Hinduism, or Buddhism is a religion? The answer, of course, is no; we assume that all these traditions are *religious* traditions. Individually and combined, they illustrate what a religious tradition is and show how various religions are both different from and similar to each other across the world.

What about Confucianism? As the academic study of world religions began in the last century, ways to interpret religious traditions were created and traditions were compared and contrasted. In the various models that were developed for the interpretation of religion, Confucianism simply did not fit very well. It was not easy to describe Confucianism as a religious tradition. It seemed to lack some element that was fundamental to readily identifiable religions. Did this mean that it was not a religion, or did it mean only that the models used to interpret religion were not broad enough to incorporate the religious character of Confucianism?

In addition to the problem faced by scholars, Confucianism was often presented as nonreligious in character even in its home cultures. During the period of modernization in the early to mid-twentieth century, even though Confucianism was thoroughly rejected by progressive leaders, it was held up by many as a part of Asian tradition that appeared to be similar to the rationalism of the West, an important attribute of what the East saw as the value of the West. Buddhism and Taoism were easily identified as religions and were often viewed as mere superstitions from the past. Confucianism, on the other hand, was different. After all, the faith's founder, Confucius, had rejected superstitious beliefs, so the argument went, and therefore his system could be viewed as rational philosophy rather than religion. Thus, it could be argued that the East had its own tradition of rationalism—Confucianism—and this rationalism set the groundwork for the East's interest in and successful adoption of Westernization and modernization. The argument hinged upon the claim that Confucianism was more rational than religious. It failed to take into account the counterargument that rationalism itself can be thoroughly religious.

This tradition on the part of various scholars of viewing Confucianism as rational goes back to the teachings of Confucius himself. Several passages from Confucius's major writing, *Lun yü*, or "Analects of Confucius," demonstrate the complexity of the issue. In one passage, Confucius is asked about spirits. He replies by saying that one should respect the spirits but keep them at a distance. In another passage, he is asked about death. He replies that he knows nothing of life, so how can he know anything about death? Surprisingly, a number of scholars have claimed that these responses indicate that Confucius was an agnostic, since he appeared to show little belief in the world of spirits and no clear belief in life after death. As a result, it has frequently been concluded that Confucianism is a rational tradition of thought, most frequently described as a form of humanism or social ethics, but not a religion.

A contrasting theory suggests that Confucianism is thoroughly religious, but in a way in which the tradition has not normally been interpreted. In another passage from the Analects, Confucius talks about his life from the point of view of an old man. He says that at age fifteen he set his heart on learning, at thirty he was established in his learning, at forty he had no doubts, at fifty he understood the will of Heaven, at sixty he could listen to the Way of Heaven, and at seventy he could do anything, for his actions all followed the Way of Heaven. In this brief autobiographical statement, Confucius described his life as being focused on coming to know the Way of Heaven through the process of learning. The critical element for Confucius is *T'ien*, or Heaven, the absolute moral power or structure in the universe. It is not a god per se, but rather an absolute force found within all things on Earth and throughout the universe. Confucius's intention was not only to come to know that force, but to live in a way that emulated its power. Because Heaven is an absolute power or force, the life Confucius describes can be defined as a religious life. Confucius has identified an ultimate source of authority in the universe—*T'ien*—and he is attempting to conform to its instructions.

Later Confucians continue to place emphasis upon the role of *T'ien* in their lives. Often, the ideal of the sage, or *sheng*, will be held up as the aim of learning and self-cultivation. Whereas, for Confucius, the sage was a virtuous figure of antiquity who could not exist in the present world, for later Confucians, particularly Neo-Confucians from the thirteenth century on, anyone could learn to become a sage. A sage was a person who had the ability to hear the Way of Heaven and manifest it to the world. In other words, the sage sought to understand *T'ien* and to live according to its way.

MAIN SUBDIVISIONS AND
SCHOOLS OF CONFUCIANISM

Although the basic Confucian point of view includes a belief in the centrality of *T'ien* and the goal of conforming to its way, there remain many variations across the tradition, even in this most basic teaching. Such differences emerge in the interpretation of basic Confucian writings, as well as currents of thought among the many individual thinkers over the centuries of Confucian history. The product of such differences has been the emergence of various schools of Confucian thought.

Several generalizations can be made about the development of subdivisions of Confucianism. First, if Confucian schools are compared to the divisions found within other religions, Confucians do not have any clear boundary that resembles, for example, the sharp division of Catholic Christianity from Protestantism or Sunni Islam from Shiite Islam. There may be differences of opinion within Confucianism, but they are always part of a mutually inclusive path of learning, not starkly contrasting claims about truth. In this respect, Confucian subdivisions may more closely resemble the separation between Hindu or Buddhist schools of thought than Western models of religion.

Second, the subdivisions and schools of Confucianism generally follow historical developments within Confucianism's country of origin, China. Traditionally, Confucianism was associated with Chinese high culture, which had a profound influence upon the countries that surrounded China. In many respects, China's effect was far-reaching and resulted in the adaptation of Chinese culture by other places. Although evidence of some other cultural settings may be seen at times in Confucianism, by and large it is the events within China that are mirrored in the Confucianism of Korea, Japan, and Southeast Asia. Probably the most notable exception to this rule would be the role that Shinto plays in influencing certain aspects of Japanese Confucianism, rather than Confucianism influencing Shinto. Even here, however, the resulting impact does not substantially change the character of Confucianism that is found in Japan.

By looking, then, at major historical developments in China, one can better understand the subdivisions of the broader Confucian tradition. The major schools of Confucianism include Classical Confucianism, Han Confucianism, Neo-Confucianism (divided into the School of Principle and the School of Mind), and Ch'ing Confucianism.

CLASSICAL CONFUCIANISM

Classical Confucianism is the name given to the founding period of the tradition. It includes Confucius (551–479 B.C.) and his disciples, as well as several of the major early Confucian thinkers, such as Hsün Tzu (c. 298–230 B.C.) and Meng Tzu, or Mencius (c. 371–289 B.C.). Classical Confucianism also incorporates certain writings, including the texts *Ta hsüeh*, or "Great Learning," and *Chung yung*, or "Doctrine of the Mean."

Confucianism developed from the tradition of the *ju*, a class of people who already existed at the time of Confucius. The *ju* were principally employed as archivists and were responsible for the preservation, transmission, and teaching of the earliest literary sources from Chinese culture. The texts they preserved became the focal point for the development of early Confucian teachings.

MENCIUS AND KING HUI OF LIANG

The first passage of the writings of Mencius (371–289 B.C.) tells the story of Mencius's discussion with King Hui of the state of Liang. As Confucius had done before him, Mencius traveled from state to state, trying to convince the rulers of his day to adopt the ways of virtue of the ancient sage rulers. Mencius lived in an age of even greater civil strife than that of Confucius, a period of time called the Warring States Period (480–221 B.C.). Because of an increase in contention between the states and open civil war, the rulers were even more desperate for advice on how to protect their own territories and perhaps defeat their enemies as well.

> Mencius saw King Hui of Liang. The king said, "So venerable an elder, having come a thousand *li*, and not considering that too far, must surely have some means to profit our state?" Mencius replied, "Why must the king speak of profit? There are humaneness and rightness, that is all. If the king says, 'How can I profit my state?' the officers will say, 'How can I profit my house?' and the gentlemen and the common people will say, 'How can I profit my person?' Those above and those below will be competing with one another for profit, and the state will be imperiled. . . . It has never happened that one given to humaneness abandons his parents, or that one given to rightness subordinates the interests of his lord. The king should speak of humaneness and rightness. Why is it necessary to speak of profit?"*

Mencius met with the same reaction Confucius had. His agenda was different from what the kings wanted to hear. Mencius's aim was to persuade the rulers to adopt the teachings of the ancient sages in order to bring peace and order to the world. His advice was not to go after the narrow interests of the state, but to seek the moral way offered by the teachings of the ancient sage rulers. Specifically, thoughts of profit, or *li*, represented only the interests of the individual; *jen*—humaneness, and *i*—righteousness or rightness, on the other hand, represented the moral integrity of all people's interests. If the king wanted to be a true ruler, he had to act from a basis of moral values, not selfish desires.

* William Theodore de Bary and Irene Bloom, comp., *Sources of Chinese Tradition*, 2nd ed., vol. 1, New York: Columbia University Press, 1999, pp. 116–117.

These first teachings focused on both the ideas and practices of the ancients as they had been recorded in classical literature. The ideas were based on belief in a moral universe under the authority of *T'ien*. The common person and ruler alike were expected to learn and cultivate their moral natures so as to conform to the Way of Heaven. The methods of doing this primarily involved the performance of *li*, the ritual or propriety of the ancients. The Confucians were experts in these ancient codes of ritual practice and believed they were just as important as the ideas of the ancients because the performance of ritual symbolized the order of the Way of Heaven.

Confucius referred to himself as a transmitter of this tradition. He saw his role as one of teaching—based on the ancient literature—a path of moral learning, conduct, and ritual practice in an otherwise chaotic world. Other early Confucians developed beliefs based on the ideas of Confucius himself, elaborating and expanding on his basic moral foundation. As the Chou Dynasty (1122–221 B.C.) slowly disintegrated, and civil strive increased among powerful and independent states, the need for these teachings became even more obvious to the Confucians. The focus of all of Classical Confucianism lay in understanding the Way of *T'ien*, which emphasized the need for moral education for individuals and the establishment of moral rule to bring peace and order to the world.

HAN CONFUCIANISM

Han Confucianism, so-called because of its correspondence with the Han Dynasty (206 B.C.–A.D. 220), saw Confucianism officially established as the orthodox ideology of the Chinese state. The Han Dynasty was a relatively lengthy period of stability, and Confucians made great progress in winning recognition for the role they could play in bringing order to the state and its institutions, both in terms of state ideology and ceremony. Confucians were recruited by the government to serve as advisors, and their influence often played a major role in the formulation of state policy. Confucianism's connection to state ceremony stemmed from the Confucians' expertise as archivists of the ancient ritual codes. In a society where ritual was seen as a critical component in the order of the world, the ruler sought out those with knowledge about ritual to ensure that the state's conduct was appropriate. The emperor, who was known as the Son of Heaven, was responsible for both the teachings and practice that would bring peace and stability to his domain. That is, it was his duty to create a society that lived according to the Way of Heaven, and thus lived with the blessing of Heaven.

Another important part of the official establishment of Confucianism was the role assigned to it in regard to education. Such a focus was again a logical extension of the Confucians' expertise as specialists in the ancient literature that served as the basis for proper learning and practice. With the advice of Confucian advisors, the government set up a national system of education. This included the opening of the first university and a nationwide educational system. The Confucians were centrally involved in the development of this system, as well as with the content of the education offered.

It was during this same Han period that the Five Classics, the main corpus of Confucian writings, and their Confucian commentaries were established as the basis of the educational system at national, regional, and local levels. Han Confucianism is principally known for the development of extensive commentary traditions. Much of the work done by Confucians during this period was writing commentaries about the earlier classics. One tradition, called the New Text School, emphasized supernatural elements in the early records and surrounding the founding figures. The other tradition, called the Old Text School, was more important. It focused on only the human qualities of both the tradition's teachings and founders, making Confucianism into the very powerful ethical system that it has remained through the centuries.

The other major development of the Han period was the creation of the Confucian Temple, where ritual and liturgy were

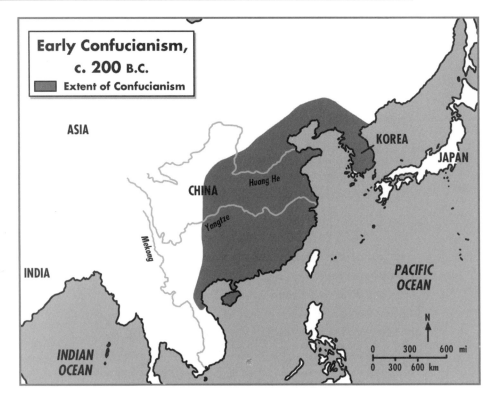

In its early years, Confucianism was confined mainly to the areas in China where Confucius and his disciples had lived and taught. Over time, however, as seen on this map, the influence of the tradition began to spread over a wide swath of Asia.

offered to Confucius and various notable figures of the tradition. Such offerings were not understood as a sacrifice to a supernatural being, but merely as a way to commemorate the teachings of Confucianism and its founders.

NEO-CONFUCIANISM
Beginning in the T'ang Dynasty (618–907) and particularly during the Northern Sung Dynasty (960–1127), Confucianism went through a major transformation. In fact, this change was significant enough to give the new form of teaching and practice its own title: Neo-Confucianism. In many ways, the subdivision's

development was a product of the advent and growth of Buddhism and liturgical Taoism (a Chinese native religion) during the preceding centuries. These traditions focused on the individual's internal processes of cultivation and learning, such as meditation, rather than on issues of the external world. Confucianism saw both of these belief systems as a major threat. They were regarded as otherworldly and not concentrated enough on the moral rectification of either the individual or the world. As a result, part of the growth of Neo-Confucianism is associated with providing a reinvigorated Confucianism that could readdress the practical needs of the world. At the same time, although they criticized Buddhism and Taoism, Confucians saw a potential model for beneficial religious life in these other traditions and began to look to their own system as a resource for more introspective forms of learning and cultivation. As a result, Neo-Confucianism was influenced by both Buddhism and Taoism. Confucians saw that Buddhists and Taoists focused first and foremost on the cultivation of their own spiritual lives. To Confucians, this was a characteristic to emulate.

The term *Neo-Confucianism* describes a very broad-based movement within the Confucian tradition. From the Sung Dynasty on, it came to characterize all of Confucianism in China and the surrounding countries that were part of the Chinese sphere of influence. It generally paid greater attention to philosophical issues than did earlier forms of Confucianism. It came to be highly focused on the goal of becoming a *sheng*, or sage. Whereas for earlier Confucianism, the sage was always a figure of the distant past, the Neo-Confucians believed it was possible for modern-day people to engage in the learning and practice necessary to actually become a sage. Such self-cultivation was a path of personal transformation. Neo-Confucians sought a fundamental moral development of the individual and believed that such development would affect all of society. They reaffirmed the nature of moral education and its import for the world. In this process, they remained highly critical of those traditions—Taoism and Buddhism—that they believed did not face the moral challenge of the rectification of the world.

Neo-Confucianism developed into two major schools during the Sung and Ming (1368–1644) dynasties. The *Li hsüeh*, or School of Principle, began during the Sung period and included major thinkers such as Chou Tun-I (1017–1073), Chang Tsai (1020–1077), Ch'eng I (1033–1107), and Chu Hsi (1130–1200). The *Hsin hsüeh*, or School of Mind, is principally associated with the Ming Dynasty and was particularly focused on the thought of the great Ming philosopher Wang Yang-ming (1472–1529). These schools reflect major differences in emphasis within the learning process. Put most simply, the School of Principle emphasized an attempt to acquire knowledge of the world—mainly through book learning and observation of nature and social relations—in order to gain an understanding of the nature of things. The School of Mind focused internally instead, believing that the study of the mind itself would reveal the nature of the world. The School of Mind recognized that action was the way in which knowledge was realized within the mind. Both schools were far more philosophically oriented than earlier types of Confucianism were.

CH'ING CONFUCIANISM

During the Ch'ing Dynasty (1644–1912), Neo-Confucianism still existed, but the dominant form of teaching represented a major shift from the Neo-Confucianism of the Sung and Ming periods. The term *Ch'ing Confucianism* refers to the schools that sought to reject much of what made up Sung and Ming Neo-Confucianism. In the eyes of the Ch'ing Confucians, the Sung and Ming developments were far too philosophical and abstract, and their forms of learning and practice were seen as too similar to those of the Buddhists and Taoists. One Ch'ing movement was called *shih hsüeh*, or Practical Learning. It focused on moral learning and emphasized the need to address the real issues and challenges

CHANG TSAI AND THE *WESTERN INSCRIPTION*

One of the great founding figures of the Neo-Confucian movement during the Sung Dynasty (960–1279), Chang Tsai (1020–1077) is best known for a short writing called *Hsi ming*, or the *Western Inscription*. It is one of the most famous works of the Confucian tradition in general and certainly the best known of all Neo-Confucian writings. Its message reflects both the great Neo-Confucian vision that believed all things throughout the universe were interconnected, as well as the tradition's statement of the moral responsibility to care for all things in the world. No one is excluded from this requirement. It captures the essential Confucian concept of the unity of the individual with all Heaven and Earth:

> Heaven is my father and Earth is my mother, and even such a small creature as I finds an intimate place in their midst. Therefore that which extends throughout the universe I regard as my body and that which directs the universe I consider as my nature. All people are my brothers and sisters, and all things are my companions. The great ruler [the emperor] is the eldest son of my parents [Heaven and Earth], and the great ministers are his stewards. Respect the aged—this is the way to treat them as elders should be treated. Show affection toward the orphaned and the weak—this is the way to treat them as the young should be treated. The sage identifies his virtue with that of Heaven and Earth, and the worthy is the best [among the children of Heaven and Earth]. Even those who are tired and infirm, crippled or sick, those who have no brothers or children, wives or husbands, are all my brothers who are in distress and have no one to turn to. When the time comes, to keep himself from harm—this is the care of a son. To rejoice in Heaven and have no anxiety—this is filiality at its purest. One who disobeys [the principle of Heaven] violates virtue. One who destroys humanity . . . is a robber. One who promotes evil lacks [moral] capacity. But one who puts his moral nature into practice and brings his physical existence to complete fulfillment can match [Heaven and Earth]. . . . In life I follow and serve [Heaven and Earth]. In death I will be at peace.*

* William Theodore de Bary and Irene Bloom, comp., *Sources of Chinese Tradition*, 2nd ed., vol. 1, New York: Columbia University Press, 1999, pp. 683–684.

17 ARTICLE CONSTITUTION OF PRINCE SHOTOKU

In the early years of the development of Japanese society and culture, Shotoku Taishi (573–621), or Prince Shotoku, played a key role in incorporating many elements of Chinese civilization into Japan. Japan saw in China an advanced and very old culture that had a number of important features that might benefit the much younger and still developing Japanese nation. To Prince Shotoku, there was especially great benefit to be found in adopting models of governmental and societal structure from China, which represented the breadth of Chinese learning. His 17 Article Constitution became one of the most important documents in early Japanese history; it served as a guide for the establishment of Japanese government and society during its critical founding stages.

The 17 Article Constitution is a basic guide for government and society based upon Chinese traditions. Its guiding principles had their foundations in Chinese ways of thought, principally Buddhism and Confucianism. Prince Shotoku himself was a devout Buddhist and a very accomplished scholar of Buddhist scripture. Because of his religious beliefs, he saw Buddhism as the final refuge for all humankind and advised that all worldly concerns be considered against the backdrop of the quest for enlightenment. Such a position did not, however, prevent him from seeing the importance of creating a harmonious society devoted to the betterment of all people. In this goal, he grounded his teachings in Confucianism.

The Confucian principles of the 17 Article Constitution focused on creating a model for the moral governing of society. The people were supposed to look to imperial rule as the source of this moral rule. They were to see the benefit of following the goals of society at large rather than their own partisan interests. Every level of the government was expected to act in moral ways for the benefit of the people as a whole. Focus was placed on the harmony within society as a whole, with the understanding that such harmony can only be achieved by acting in moral ways toward every individual. Though these principles are quite general and idealistic, the work has nonetheless remained a central element of Japanese government and society, reflecting Japan's deep commitment to Confucian teachings and values.

of the world, rather than the lofty pursuit of philosophical and almost unworldly goals.

The second form of Ch'ing Confucianism is called *k'ao-cheng*—Evidential Research or Textual Criticism. It, too, rejected what it perceived as the abstract nature of the beliefs of the Sung and Ming Neo-Confucians. In many respects, such as its close attention to ancient texts, it sought a return to earlier forms of Confucianism, particularly as found in the commentary tradition of Han Confucianism and the simple ethical teachings at the roots of Classical Confucianism.

PARALLEL DEVELOPMENTS

As these developments were taking place in China, they were also occurring nearly simultaneously throughout all the other cultures that were influenced by Confucianism. Across East and Southeast Asia, the study of Confucianism was considered an essential part of learning. With the long-standing influence of Chinese culture throughout Asia, the introduction of Classical and Han Confucianism came about early in each of these cultures. With the advent of Neo-Confucianism in China, Korea and Japan quickly followed in assimilating and developing equivalent models of Neo-Confucian learning and practice. We have only to look to the Chosen Dynasty (1392–1910) in Korea to see the prominent role given to the School of Principle of Neo-Confucianism, particularly under the great Korean Neo-Confucian philosopher Yi T'oegye (1501–1570). In Japan, it is during the Tokugawa Period (1603–1868) in particular that virtually all major developments of Chinese Neo-Confucianism took place. The Ch'ing schools of Confucianism had an influence as well.

By the dawn of the modern age, the Confucian tradition had gone through rich and complex developments that stemmed from its Chinese roots, but were nonetheless creatively expressed across a range of Asian cultures. Confucianism's fate as it encountered modernization and Westernization would appear to many to be the end of its story. We must not, however, prejudge its destiny. It may well be the case that Confucianism's last chapter is not yet written.

2

The Story of Confucius

Confucius, at home in his native village,
was simple and unassuming in manner,
as though he did not trust himself to speak.
But when in the ancestral temple or at Court
he speaks readily, though always
choosing his words with due caution.

—Analects 10:1

The story of Confucius begins in the declining centuries of the lengthy Chinese period known as the Chou Dynasty, during a time called the Spring and Autumn Period (722–481 B.C.; the era took its name from the chronicle that covered the history of the state of Lu during this era). At this time, the central authority of the Chou Dynasty was undermined and weakened. The Chou Dynasty operated with a ruler over a centralized government. With the passage of time, the power of the central government began to crumble and various states within the original centralized system became more independent. Although the central government remained in power, it became a government in name only as the states themselves controlled their own territories. In turn, the states began to compete with one another, and the result was civil war, with the aim of establishing a new central government and ruler. The age was marked by civil wars among the various states; peace was to be found nowhere in the Chinese realm. Poems from this period, found in the *Shih ching*, or Classic of Poetry, describe a world in which countless innocent people experience chaos and suffering.

Even the traditional gods were questioned as sources of mercy. Chinese religion was originally focused on ancestral cults and was under the sway of the ruling family, which projected its own ancestral figures as gods overseeing the entire realm. Thus, the Shang and Chou dynasties each had high gods, probably originally ancestral spirits, and a complex state of cult sacrifice and ritual that worshiped these figures. For succeeding generations, the chaos continued to increase. The final period of the Chou Dynasty was known as the Warring States Period (480–221 B.C.), an accurate description of the condition endured by the Chinese people of the time.

Within this setting, a very great intellectual creativity was born, and the major schools of Chinese thought came into existence. This development became known as the Hundred Schools of Thought. There were not literally a hundred schools, but there *were* many creative thinkers who formulated different ways of looking at the world and different paths for humankind to follow.

The creation of these schools of thought may be seen as a direct response to the chaos of the time. What seems to have happened is that, as the chaos of the time worsened, the gods seemed to play less and less of a role. The philosophical schools arose to fill the void by providing ways in which the realm or the individual might be able to cope. In a way, each school addressed the same questions: How can humankind move past chaos to a time of peace and order? What is the proper path for humankind to follow to create a peaceful and orderly world? Though many answers were offered, the best known of the so-called Hundred Schools were Confucianism and Taoism.

Confucianism and Taoism each addressed the chaos of the times and responded in very different ways. For the Taoist, the way to order lay in retreating from the ordinary world and living out one's years in a quiet, peaceful setting. For the Confucian, on the other hand, the answer lay in addressing the unrest of the time directly by transforming the chaos to order. The Confucian determination was to engage the world and offer suggestions for ways to bring about a state of peace and harmony. Across the history of the tradition, the lives of many Confucians follow the model of engagement and commitment to improve the world. This model applies especially well to the founder of the tradition, Confucius.

THE LIFE OF CONFUCIUS

Confucius is known in Chinese as either *K'ung Tzu* or *K'ung Fu-tzu*, which may be translated as "Master K'ung" or "Great Master K'ung." These names originate with his family name, which was K'ung. His first name was Ch'iu, with the polite or courtesy name of Chung-ni. Thus, he was K'ung Ch'iu or K'ung Chung-ni. The Latinized name "Confucius," derived from K'ung Fu-tzu, was given to him by Jesuit priests when they arrived in China centuries later.

Very little is known of Confucius's life. Biographical details are limited to only a few very brief accounts. Even in the collection of his sayings, *Lun yü*, or Analects of Confucius, the most important source of information about Confucius, his disciples, and his thought, little light is shed on details of his life. What we do know is that Confucius's family seems originally to have been of the low nobility from the state of Sung. The family left Sung and immigrated to the very small state of Lu. By the time of Confucius's birth, the family was in dire straits. Confucius's father died when Confucius was still an infant, and his mother died when he was a teenager. Little else is known about his childhood, though there is some indication that he married in his late teenage years.

The next available information about Confucius refers to his holding various minor governmental positions in the state of Lu. Nothing is known about how he came to acquire these positions or what kind of education or training he had in his youth that would have qualified him to be a governmental official. Confucius makes a reference to beginning his education at the age of fifteen, but no details are given about the content of that learning.

There is some indication that Confucius spent several years in the state of Ch'i but then returned to Lu, probably in 515 B.C. After a period of learning and teaching, he again emerged as a candidate for several governmental positions. Beginning in 500 B.C., he is said to have held a series of higher-level posts in the state of Lu, including vice minister of works, minister of justice, and finally, prime minister. His rise up the ladder of success came to a rapid end with his resignation in 497 B.C. There is a story associated with his resignation. Supposedly, when the ruler of Ch'i heard that the leader of Lu had employed Confucius, the ruler of Ch'i sent eighty beautiful women to the leader of Lu as a diversion from his rulership. This upset Confucius, who resigned in protest. Whether or not the tale is true, Confucius did not serve in a government post again.

Following his resignation, Confucius began what is probably the most famous period of his life. For about the next fourteen years, he went from state to state, seeking an audience with each of the state rulers. He traveled with a number of his disciples, at times under dangerous circumstances, to find opportunities to give advice to the leaders of his day on ways to transform the chaos of their age to peace and order. It appears that he was able to have meetings with a number of rulers, but his advice and his teaching largely fell on deaf ears.

Confucius's suggestion was to return to the moral ways of the ancient sage kings and the virtuous rulers who had been responsible for the founding of the Chou Dynasty. He argued strenuously that there was extraordinary power in the virtue of the ancients. In fact, he believed that if a small state, such as his own state of Lu, adopted the ancient ways—moral rule in which the ruler served Heaven and governed with moral concern for his people—then it would be able to defeat even the largest and most powerful state. To the rulers of the day, who were facing the danger of increasing civil strife and military threats from their neighbors, such advice seemed to have little practicality. As a result, if his impact is measured by the adoption of his ideas, Confucius had no success whatsoever.

With no state willing to employ him or his ideas, Confucius retired to his native state of Lu in 484 B.C. and taught an increasing number of disciples until his death in 479 B.C. Accounts vary as to the number of disciples Confucius gathered around him during his life, but it is often said that he had almost three thousand disciples more than seventy of whom were considered close to him. He is also said to have edited or compiled the Five Classics, the foundational works of Chinese culture and the basic scriptural sources for the Confucian tradition. Though Confucius might be described as an apparent failure in his efforts to counsel state rulers on policy for their states, his disciples spread his teachings and began a tradition of thought and practice that has remained one of the most significant and enduring elements of Asian culture.

CONFUCIUS IN FOLKLORE

Though there is little information about most of Confucius's life in official sources, over the centuries a rich folklore has grown up about Confucius. Many of these stories are an important part of popular culture and represent the common people's understanding of Confucius. In a number of these tales, Confucius is portrayed as possessing supernatural power or being in some fashion linked to the display of such powers.

There are, for example, narratives that claim Confucius had a miraculous birth on the Ni-ch'iu Mound (the small hill where Confucius was said to be born) and also describe the magical appearance of a spring at the foot of the mound to provide Confucius's mother with water. There are said to have been portents of his birth—on the night before he was born, his mother reportedly saw fantastical animals such as the unicorn and dragon, as well as immortal musicians. There are also stories of Confucius's prediction of a flood and of supernatural dealings between him and his disciples. His birthplace in Ch'ü-fu, the site of his temple, is often believed to have extraordinary powers because it has managed to withstand many natural disasters over the years. There are said to be juniper plants both at the Confucian Temple and at the place of his birth that were able to reflect the rise and fall of dynasties by their own growth and decline. A commonly repeated story, and one that can actually be found in official sources, refers to Confucius's contentment as a child in playing with instruments used in the performance of rituals, such as bowls, cups, ladles, and other vessels—an early indication of his eventual focus on the importance of ritual to the ordering of society and the world.

Some of the official sources that depicted Confucius as someone who seemed to possess supernatural powers and abilities were written during the Han period and came to be known as the New Text School. By contrast, the sources that came to be accepted as official and orthodox, called the Old Text School, sought to portray Confucius as a human being who had no special powers. In fact, supernatural elements were eliminated almost entirely from any portrayal of Confucius, his disciples, other early Confucians, or any part of the tradition. Confucius is depicted principally as a teacher and scholar. The dominant image across the centuries has reinforced the degree to which Confucius is first and foremost a wise teacher and scholar, a loyal minister of the state, or even a sage king and uncrowned ruler—not a supernatural figure who engages in miraculous activities.

CONFUCIUS OF THE ANALECTS

The most common images of Confucius are those found in the major source of his thought, the Analects. A number of passages give the reader a sense of what Confucius was like as a person, how he interacted with his disciples, and how he was viewed by his followers. Most of the statements are very down-to-earth and

TO LEARN AND TO REPEAT WHAT ONE HAS LEARNED

There is no more famous passage in all of Confucian literature than the first passage of the Confucian Analects, the chief teachings of Confucius, the founder of the tradition. The passage reads:

> The Master [Confucius] said, "To learn, and at due times to practice what one has learned, is that not also a pleasure? To have friends come from afar, is that not also a joy? To go unrecognized, yet without being embittered, is that not also to be a noble person?"*

This passage set the tone for the rest of the writings of Confucius. It is very straightforward. There is nothing complex, nothing abstract; it is just Confucius talking about the role of learning. Despite its simplicity, within this statement lies the very heart of Confucian teaching: To learn means to develop an understanding of the ways of the sage rulers of antiquity, and from them, the Way of T'ien.

For Confucius, learning was not enough in and of itself; it had to go on to practice. People learned the moral ways of the sages of antiquity and then practiced those moral ways in everyday life. The measure of learning could be seen in the ability to practice what one has learned. Confucians were supposed to spread their learning and appreciate the simple joys of sharing moments with friends. They also had to recognize that much of the world did not want to hear about the moral ways of the sages of antiquity. To Confucius, it was of no concern to go unrecognized. The tradition's focus is, instead, upon becoming a noble person, someone whose every thought and action is the product of his or her moral nature and a reflection of the depth of Heaven's Way.

* William Theodore de Bary and Irene Bloom, comp., *Sources of Chinese Tradition*, 2nd ed., vol. 1, New York: Columbia University Press, 1999, p. 45.

reveal a kindly and human-centered man who cared deeply about those who followed him, about the state of the world, and about the learning of the ancients.

Confucius said that he needed only the simplest of things to live—merely coarse food for his diet, a drink of water, and a folded arm for a pillow. He spoke of his passion for learning, which caused him to forget to eat, to forget his worries, and to forget that he was growing old. His disciples described him as gentle yet strong, dignified without being abrasive or arrogant, courteous yet relaxed.

Confucius expressed his concern that when hunting, one should not hunt in a fashion that would take advantage of the animals. He said that one should not fish with a net or shoot at a nesting bird. The issue is one of fairness: If hunting is to be done justly, it must be a "competition" between hunter and prey—the animal must have some chance of eluding the hunter.

Another passage in the Analects describes a fire at a stable. A disciple comments that when he learned of the fire, Confucius asked if anyone had been hurt, but did not inquire about the safety of the horses. Some interpretations have suggested that human life alone was his priority.

In another passage, when the suggestion is made that a person might retreat from the world in times of chaos, Confucius responds by saying that he cannot live with the birds and animals. He is, after all, a man, and to fulfill his role as a man he must live in a human community. If that community is flawed, then it is his duty to introduce the learning necessary to bring peace and order.

There are also passages where Confucius appears to give a sense of his mission to the world. He tells his disciples at one point, after the last founding figure of the Chou Dynasty dies, that the teaching of the ancients seems to depend only upon him. Without his success, the teaching itself will be destroyed. He looks to *T'ien* as the source of the protection he needs to propagate the ancient ways, saying that its survival rests entirely with Heaven itself.

Confucius also says several times that only Heaven knows him. That is, the world has not recognized him and does not comprehend the importance of his mission, but at least Heaven does understand. Despite his reliance upon *T'ien*, however, he no longer seems to believe that Heaven is guiding his efforts after Yen Hui, his favorite disciple, dies. Confucius, who falls into a state of utter despair, can only say that heaven has left him.

Still, when all is said and done, Confucius reveals himself to be a person who remains committed to learning the Way of Heaven and sharing it with others to help improve the world. His philosophical repose in learning the Way of Heaven is suggested when he says that, if he can hear the Way of *T'ien* in the morning, then he can die at peace in the evening.

CONFUCIUS AS FOUNDER AND TRANSMITTER

We identify Confucius as the founder of the Confucian tradition, yet when he spoke of his role, he referred to himself merely as a transmitter of the learning of the sage kings of antiquity and the virtuous founders of the Chou Dynasty. In this sense, in his own mind, he was not an originator or creator of a tradition. His teachings were not his own. He was simply bringing them to his own generation from the ancient periods of Chinese history. His sources for these teachings were the literary classics that purported to represent the ancient periods. These are the works that Confucius is said to have had some direct role in, either through editing or compiling them. Although such stories are usually discounted in modern scholarship, it is important to understand Confucius's role in order to explain the authority vested in him as founder by the Confucian tradition itself.

Though we know very little about Confucius's life, it is generally assumed that he was part of a group or class of people referred to as the *ju*, or archivists. In many ways, these people were the librarians of their day. They collected and preserved literary works from the past. Confucius's knowledge of these works and his possible role in editing or compiling them would indicate the degree to which he was a *ju*.

There is more behind the development of Confucianism, however, than Confucius's claim that he is a transmitter. Although in

Chinese the term *Confucianism* is most frequently translated as *ju hsüeh*, or the "learning of the ju," and the term *Confucianism* itself is a Western creation, nonetheless Confucius has been intimately associated with the founding of the tradition through its entire history. Later Confucians, after all, referred to Confucius as the founder of the tradition. What is it about Confucius that makes him the founder of a tradition that already existed and of which he was a part?

As he transmitted the ancient learning, Confucius brought a modern relevance for his own generation to the teachings of the ancients, and as it turned out, for several thousands of years of succeeding generations. He taught that the ancients provided ideas that could be applied to his own generation—by implementing the teachings into rulership and making the ruler lead in a moral way. This would bring about peace and order. He took these old teachings and decided that they were inherently valuable, not just because they represented the work of the ancients, but because they included universal truths about the way people should live, how they should interact with each other, how society should be governed, and how humans should follow the moral authority found in the universe, the Way of *T'ien*.

Confucius saw the ancient works as providing a template for humankind to follow. Tremendous authority was vested in the sages of antiquity, in part because the records of their rule suggested that they had governed in moral ways and that they had established peace in the world. In addition, the sages were seen as a direct link to *T'ien* itself. The sages, after all, were viewed as people who heard the Way of Heaven and showed it to the world. The Five Classics were the records of the sages' thoughts and actions. Confucius said that the learning found in the Five Classics formed the foundation for understanding the Way of *T'ien*, and with the acquisition of such learning, the individual and the world could be transformed to moral order that conformed to the Way of Heaven.

There is another very important sense in which Confucius was a founder and not just a transmitter. In addition to establishing the learning of the sages as the basis for the moral transformation of his own age, Confucius also suggested that learning was possible for anyone with the motivation and energy to pursue it. Though this may seem like a minor point, his commitment to making education available to all people is one of the most important innovations that Confucius brought to the traditions of the learning of the *ju*.

The goal of the learning process that Confucius advocates allows a student to become a *chün tzu*, or "noble person." Before Confucius, a *chün tzu* had to be noble by birth. A common person could not rise to the ranks of nobility. Confucius talks at great length about pursuing the learning necessary to become a *chün tzu*. Is he talking about trying to lift oneself into the ranks of social nobility? The answer is no. Rather, he sees the *chün tzu* as someone of personal nobility, someone who possesses the virtue that comes from moral learning and training. Thanks to Confucius, the *chün tzu* no longer had any association with nobility by birth, but was connected instead with moral training. According to Confucius, anyone with enough diligence can become a *chün tzu*—which is newly defined as a superior, exemplary, or profound person.

The change initiated by Confucius in the meaning of this term has demonstrated to most Confucians over the centuries that Confucius was a true founder. Not only did he begin a tradition based on the belief that learning would transform an individual into a moral person and the world into a moral order, but most importantly, he said that anyone was capable of pursuing this goal. Confucius was breaking down the class society of the ancients in which learning was reserved for those of noble birth.

A RELIGIOUS FOUNDER?

We have already considered the issue of Confucianism as a religious tradition. We have seen the ambiguity that surrounds the issue and the degree to which the tradition has often been presented as a form of humanism or social ethics rather than a religion. Through quotes from Confucius himself, we have seen

both the grounds for claim of a nonreligious and largely human-
istic tradition as well as the ways in which the tradition might be
considered religious. Just as Confucianism is very different from
other belief systems, Confucius himself is perceived differently
from the founding figures of many other religious traditions in
several ways.

First, where a founder of a religious tradition is often seen as
someone who has received some direct revelation of a message
for humankind from God, Confucius is portrayed as a transmitter of writings that represent the human rulers of antiquity, not
God or some other divine source. Second, where a founder may
be seen to have an array of supernatural powers or incidents
surrounding his life, Confucius has been deliberately portrayed
as lacking these characteristics. With the exception of legends
at the folklore level, such material has played no role in the
Confucian tradition. Third, most religious founders are
focused on a state that might be described as the salvation of
humankind. Such salvation could consist in moving the individual from his or her present condition to some ultimate place,
be it the Christian heaven or Buddhist nirvana. Confucius, on
the other hand, is only concerned with the moral transformation
of the physical world in which we currently live—not with
attempting to reach a better place after death. Confucius does
not bear any message that encourages people to think beyond
their own lives. Keep in mind his answer to the question about
the nature of death: Confucius says he does not yet know life, so
how could he know death? Does this make Confucius a founder
of a tradition that is not religious? No—the answer continues
to lie in his perception of *T'ien* as the absolute moral power of
the universe. He models his life on the Way of Heaven and
he encourages others to do so, too. The difference is that the
religious meaning is found within life itself, not in some state
after death. Although there may be such a state, it is not part of
Confucian thought.

3

Confucian Scripture

> The Master said, "Behave in office as though
> you were receiving an important guest.
> Employ the people as though you were
> considering an important sacrifice.
> What you do not like yourself do not do to others."
>
> —Analects 12:2

When the word *scripture* is used in a religious tradition, it usually refers to a work that is believed to come from God or some other divine source. Most frequently, scripture is thought of as a work divinely revealed to humankind that assumes a position of tremendous authority for the adherents of a particular religion. Authority is vested in scripture because it is considered a source of deep and profound knowledge— knowledge that goes well beyond the kind of ordinary information one might find in a newspaper, magazine, or book. Scripture contains knowledge that is often believed to reveal the deeper meaning and purpose of life itself. It therefore may be viewed as a blueprint for how people are supposed to live. Such works are regarded as very special writings and are treated with a high level of respect and devotion. They often become guidebooks for an individual to follow through his or her lifetime.

The Confucian tradition has a number of writings that may be considered authoritative for adherents of the tradition. The first of these is a group of texts referred to most frequently as the Five Classics (though they are sometimes called the Six Classics). The Five Classics date from early Chinese history, predating even the first phase of Confucian tradition. They became central to the development of early, or Classical, Confucianism and remained in this role until the development of Neo-Confucianism during the Sung Dynasty. Even then, the Five Classics maintain their importance as the foundational set of writings representing what the Confucians considered the tradition they sought to preserve and teach.

The second group of writings is called the Four Books. Although each of the writings that make up this collection is of an early date, the writings were not put together until the advent of Neo-Confucianism, principally during the Sung Dynasty. From that period on and into the twentieth century, the Four Books were regarded as a critical collection of Confucian writings, both because they augmented the Five Classics and because of their value as a stand-alone set of basic teachings.

A CONFUCIAN SCRIPTURE?

As we examine various elements of the Confucian tradition, one of the questions that continues to come up is whether Confucianism is a religion at all. One of the obvious questions when discussing a religious tradition is the identification of the religion's scripture and the discussion of the central role that it plays across the faith's history. For most religions of the world, it would not be necessary to demonstrate that the foundational writings within the tradition are, in fact, scripture. Because Confucianism is still so often interpreted as a form of humanism and a code of ethics, however, it is necessary to decide whether or not the Confucian texts can be considered scripture.

There is no doubt that the Five Classics and the Four Books have played a central role for Confucianism throughout its history. The questions that arise are whether these works can be called the "scripture" of the Confucian tradition, and, if they are scripture, what that means within the Confucian context. In other words, there is sufficient discomfort with the application of the term *scripture* to Confucian writings that most authors simply do not use it. They refer instead to these texts as literary or philosophical sources for the Confucian tradition.

If we choose to describe these writings as Confucian scripture, there is a certain issue that quickly comes to mind. To be scripture, writings must be regarded as religious. What about the texts of Confucianism makes them religious? If scripture is a revelation from God or even some divine source, neither set of Confucian writings appears to qualify. Because the writings do not have an obvious connection to a source of religious authority, they have often been dismissed as religious writings. The fact remains, though, that for many adherents of the tradition, the writings *are* religious. The question to be answered is what the basis is for Confucianism's understanding of the texts as religious works.

THE FIVE CLASSICS

The Five Classics are a collection of what are believed to be the earliest literary writings from Chinese culture. Though the dates of the various Classics are uncertain, tradition holds that they originated in the earliest periods of Chinese history, and they are often associated with founding figures or sage rulers from China's distant past. This past is thought to have begun with certain ancient cultural heroes in the late third millennium B.C. They were followed by the wise rulers Yao, Shun, and Yü, who bridge the gap toward early dynastic history, with the Hsia Dynasty in the nineteenth and eighteenth centuries B.C., the Shang in the seventeenth century B.C., and finally the Chou Dynasty, beginning in the twelfth century B.C. It is not until the Chou Dynasty that scholars actually have historical evidence of the Five Classics' existence. Nonetheless, in the traditional view of China's past, this construction of the ancient periods was considered critical and, as a result, it made sense that the Five Classics would themselves be a product of these ancient times.

Key to understanding a group of writings such as the Five Classics as scripture is an understanding of the term *Classic* or *Book*. The word *Classic* or *Book*—*ching* in Chinese—stems from the handicraft of weaving. It refers to the threads that run lengthwise through a piece of cloth, what is called the "warp." From this origin, the word has come to mean "that which runs throughout something," whether a piece of cloth or an entire culture. It can mean a rule, a law, or a norm—something that can be found throughout a culture and ties it together. When this definition is applied to a particular text, it implies that the writing is a work that provides a continuing meaning for a culture by setting down basic rules or standards. Confucian writings are almost always translated as "Classic," showing that the texts have fundamental meaning for the culture.

The same term *ching* is also used for both Buddhist and Taoist writings in East Asia. When it is used in those traditions, it is translated as "scripture" rather than "Classic" or "Book." Why is there a difference in the translation of the same term when it is used in Buddhism and Taoism as opposed to when it is used in Confucianism? Generally, the answer is that the writings of Buddhism and Taoism are considered scripture because they find their origins in an easily recognized religious source—a god or gods, who are believed to have revealed the works to humankind. With Confucianism, on the other hand, there is no immediate sense of a god or gods, and therefore, it is more difficult to identify a religious source for the writings.

The creators of the Five Classics are said to be ancient sages, figures who were supposed to have lived at the beginning of Chinese culture. The term for "sage," *sheng*, is important to understand if we want to fully grasp the meaning of the Five Classics. The Chinese character for *sage* literally means "the one who hears and manifests." The earliest explanations given suggested that the sage "hears" the Way of *T'ien* and then acts, or "manifests," in the world, based upon what he has heard. *T'ien* is not a god for the Confucians, though its origin may well be a god-like figure. Instead, *T'ien* is the supreme moral force that is believed to underlie the universe. Thus, upon "hearing" this source of supreme moral authority, the sage enacts what he or she has heard in the world. The "Classics" or "Books" are the written records of what the sages have heard of Heaven's Way and, therefore, serve as a blueprint for how people should live.

The Five Classics include: *I ching*, or Classic or Book of Changes; *Shu ching*, or Classic or Book of History; *Shih ching*, or Classic or Book of Poetry; *Li chi*, or Book of Rites; and *Ch'un-ch'iu*, or Spring and Autumn Annals. There is also reference to a Sixth Classic, a lost text, on music.

In traditional accounts, not generally accepted by modern scholars, Confucius is given some central role in the composition and editing, or at least the transmission, of these works. As Confucianism was established during the Han period, much of the tradition focused on the Classics and their meaning. The official title given to those who studied and taught the Classics was *wu-ching po-shih*, or "Scholars of the Five

Classics." As time passed, legends about Confucius's own role in the creation of the Classics increased until he came to be regarded within traditional Confucianism not only as a transmitter of the Classics, but as one of their writers, too.

The *I ching*, or Classic of Changes, appears to have origins that are quite ancient, certainly in the Shang Dynasty (1766–1122 B.C.). It is a work of divination—that is, it contains questions put to gods and ancestral spirits about the affairs of the living. The questions ask whether certain actions will be auspicious or inauspicious, or ask about the nature of the guidance of the world of spirits. Much later, commentaries, called "wings," were added to the original text. These provided a more philosophical meaning to the work, suggesting that change in the universe proceeds in an ordered fashion and that humankind, by following the guidance of the text, can understand this change and live according to the Way of *T'ien*, thereby living a harmonious life.

The *Shu ching*, the Classic or Book of History, is a collection of various writings representing statements by rulers from the sage kings to the founders of the Chou Dynasty (1122–221 B.C.). Though there are serious scholarly questions about whether the records are authentic, the real importance of the work lies in its portrayal of guiding statements from the venerated rulers of ancient China. Again, it is necessary to understand that these are not just the statements of any rulers of the day, but of rulers who were judged to have been virtuous. Virtue was viewed as a mark that proved one had heard and acted on the Way of *T'ien*. These rulers governed with religious understanding and authority. If these rulers are believed to have possessed religious authority, then their writings become a source of religious authority for both early and later Chinese culture. History is not just history, but a record of those who have heard the Way of *T'ien*. As such, history is sacred.

The *Shih ching*, or Classic or Book of Poetry, is a collection of more than three hundred poems collected from what appears to be a variety of sources. They quite clearly date from the early Chou Dynasty. Although the collection of poetry has been subject to a wide variation of interpretation, Confucians across the centuries have in general seen the poems as representing moral lessons, even in cases where a particular poem appears to be nothing more than an expression of love between a man and a woman. If the work is to be treated as a "Classic," from the Confucian perspective, it is necessary to find within it some fundamental indication of the moral fiber of humankind and a pattern for the ways in which people should live. Such a pattern, from the Confucian point of view, reflects the moral authority of the Way of *T'ien*, as interpreted by the sages of antiquity.

The Classic or Book of Rites is generally considered a collection of several works. The *Li chi* is the best known of these.

CONFUCIAN POETRY

The *Shih ching*, or Classic or Book of Poetry, is the most famous collection of poetry in all of Chinese literature. It is one of the Five Classics. When asked whether the poetry is Confucian, many people will respond that it includes many themes and topics, and focuses little on moral teachings directly. From the Confucian point of view, on the other hand, the collection is regarded as brilliant poetry precisely because it *does* exemplify Confucian teachings and values. Confucius himself commented that there was not a single word in the work that is anything other than morally good. There are, of course, many poems that would seem to have little or nothing to do with moral goodness, but even in those cases, Confucians have argued that they are allusions of moral lessons. The following may be seen as an example of the type of poem found in the work that would be judged to display moral value for the Confucians:

1
Cold is the north wind,
the snow falls thick.
If you are kind and love me
take my hand and we'll go together.
You are modest, you are slow,
but oh, we must hurry!

In general, these texts focus upon rituals and their importance to the maintenance of order for society and the individual. Some of the writings are very detailed descriptions of particular rites; others discuss the broader meaning of ritual as a component of the order of the universe. In each case, the meaning of ritual is believed to reflect the moral structure of the universe in general. These are rituals set in the context of the authority of Heaven, as described by the ancient sages. This relation of ritual to the sages of antiquity suggests the degree to which such rites become a fulfillment or enactment of the order of the Way of Heaven, and therefore are very religious.

The *Ch'un-ch'iu*, or, as it is usually called, the Spring and Autumn Annals, is a record of events from the small state of

2
Fierce is the north wind,
the snow falls fast.
If you are kind and love me,
take my hand and we'll go home together.
You are modest, you are slow,
but oh, we must hurry!

3
Nothing redder than the fox,
nothing blacker than the crow.
If you are kind and love me,
take my hand and we'll ride together.
You are modest, you are slow,
but oh, we must hurry! *

Whatever its original meaning, a poem like this one was, to Confucians, a statement of moral concern and commitment. In this case, the poem is not just a simple love song as it appears to be, but instead echoes the cries of people suffering from political oppression who are encouraging each other to seek political asylum in a state where human relations are governed according to moral ways.

* William Theodore de Bary and Irene Bloom, comp., *Sources of Chinese Tradition*, 2nd ed., vol. 1, New York: Columbia University Press, 1999, p. 40.

Lu, the native land of Confucius, from 722 to 479 B.C. The style of writing is very terse, which led later Confucians to compose several major commentaries that have subsequently accompanied the work. Why would a chronicle of events from a single state over a very limited period of time be raised to the status of one of the select Classics? The answer lies in the significance attributed to the fact that it is a chronicle of the state in which Confucius was born and raised. If one views history as a display of the moral nature of the Way of *T'ien*, then the events in the state of Lu take on an even greater significance, simply because of the importance of Confucius to Chinese history. The work becomes the sacred history of the state of Lu.

Finally, there are references to a sixth Classic, the Classic of Music. No separate work by that name exists today, though there is a shorter piece of writing within the ritual Classic that addresses the topic of music. It is primarily a discussion of the philosophical meaning of music, suggesting the degree to which music is built upon harmony, which is, in turn, considered an underlying feature of the universe in general. Like ritual, harmony is believed to be part of the foundation of all things in the universe and an indication of the moral structure of the universe as found in the Way of *T'ien*.

As the written records of Heaven's Way, the Five Classics may be regarded as religious sources of authority—or scripture—for the adherents of the Confucian tradition. They originated with *T'ien*, Heaven, the supreme moral authority of the universe, and came into being through the efforts of the sages of antiquity. As scripture, the writings were held in great devotion and respect and have continued to play a major role, even to contemporary times.

As the Confucian tradition evolved, a second collection of writings also emerged as central to the Confucian tradition. In some ways, this second collection at times has eclipsed the importance of the Five Classics, although it never substituted for their basic authority.

THE FOUR BOOKS

By the T'ang Dynasty (A.D. 618–907), the Five Classics had been established as Confucian orthodoxy for the state and for the individual. As it turned out, not all Confucians were content with the particular meanings that had been given to the Classics, however, and many sought to find their own understandings of the texts. What grew out of this discontent in part was the development of Neo-Confucianism, which emerged during the Sung period and essentially represents the mainstream of Confucian thought from the Sung Dynasty to the present day.

A large part of the Neo-Confucian agenda was to challenge the role and meaning of the traditional Classics, placing a greater emphasis on more personal and philosophical meanings than the standard interpretations did. People were still writing commentaries on the Classics, but these were now more focused on individual interpretations rather than traditional understandings of the texts. As this trend continued, the Classics became, in a way, almost secondary to the individual interpretations of the Neo-Confucian thinkers. These Confucians saw the Classics as a path to individual understanding rather than a collection of fixed orthodox meanings.

With this tendency to see the Classics as a vehicle for individual interpretation came the establishment of a new grouping of writings. The writings themselves were not new. In fact, some of them came from the Classics themselves. What was new was the grouping itself and the inclusion of major writings by the founding figures of the Confucian tradition, bringing them to a position of prominence alongside Confucius himself. This set of writings is called the Four Books. It was principally the product of the great Neo-Confucian philosopher Chu Hsi (A.D. 1130–1200), who was responsible for bringing the works together and suggesting that they represented a new approach to Confucian learning.

The Four Books are composed of *Ta hsüeh*, or Great Learning;

Lun yü, or Confucian Analects; *Meng Tzu,* or Mencius; and *Chung-yung,* or Doctrine of the Mean. The Confucian Analects is the text that records the conversations and sayings of Confucius with his disciples. It is regarded as the most complete account of the founder of the Confucian tradition, Confucius. The *Meng Tzu* comprises the writings of the figure who became seen as second only to Confucius in the development of the Confucian tradition. Up to this point, Mencius had been merely one of several early Confucian thinkers. With the placement of his writings in the Four Books, he became the official interpreter of Confucius and his teachings. This elevation of Mencius was itself a major innovation that came about with the creation of the Four Books.

The Great Learning and the Doctrine of the Mean are both chapters found in the *Li chi,* or Book of Rites, one of the Five Classics. The Great Learning is a very short text that summarizes a way to bring peace to the world through individual learning and moral cultivation. It stresses the importance of moral learning as the foundation for harmony within the family, society, and the world at large. The Doctrine of the Mean is the most subtle and complex of the works found in the Four Books. It, too, stresses the importance of learning for the individual, but within a context of the entire universe, where the Way of *T'ien* is seen as underlying all things.

These works together became, for all intents and purposes, the new scriptural authority of Neo-Confucianism. Some interpreted this set of books as an approach to the Five Classics. One began study with the Four Books, and only after thoroughly comprehending their meaning did one move on to the Five Classics. On the other hand, for many Neo-Confucians, the Four Books were seen almost as a substitute for the Five Classics.

At least in practical terms, the Four Books were both the beginning and the end of the learning process in Neo-Confucianism. At times, the Four Books became more prominent than the Classics themselves, and some Neo-Confucians saw no need

THE GREAT LEARNING

The *Ta hsüeh*, or Great Learning, is one of the most important writings within the Confucian tradition. Originally a chapter in the *Li chi*, or Book of Rites, it was regarded early on as a major work and was placed by the Neo-Confucians as a separate text in the Four Books, one of the most influential collections of writings from the twelfth century to the twentieth century. The Great Learning is very short, and its message is a simple one: Peace and order in the world is ultimately dependent on the moral learning and cultivation of each individual. One cannot expect to implement moral ways in any larger setting—be it the world, the state, or the family—without first regulating personal morality. What this suggests for the Confucian is that all problems in the world must be solved through the moral transformation of the self:

> The Way of the Great Learning lies in illuminating luminous virtue, treating the people with affection, and resting in perfect goodness. Knowing where to rest, one is able to be settled; having become settled, one is able to become tranquil; having become tranquil, one is able to be at peace; being at peace, one is able to reflect; through reflection one is able to attain understanding. . . .
>
> Those in antiquity who wished to illuminate luminous virtue throughout the world would first govern their states; wishing to govern their states, they would first bring order to their families; wishing to bring order to their families, they would first cultivate their own persons; wishing to cultivate their own persons, they would first rectify their minds; wishing to rectify their minds, they would first make their thoughts sincere; wishing to make their thoughts sincere, they would first extend their knowledge. The extension of knowledge lies in the investigation of things. . . .
>
> From the son of Heaven to ordinary people, all, without exception, should regard cultivating the person as the root . . . This is called knowing the root; this is called the perfection of knowledge.*

---

* William Theodore de Bary and Irene Bloom, comp., *Sources of Chinese Tradition*, 2nd ed., vol. 1, New York: Columbia University Press, 1999, pp. 330–331.

to study the Classics at all. For many, the Four Books were all that was needed to practice Confucianism. Chu Hsi even set the order of the works to represent a complete path of learning. One began with the Great Learning, to set the framework for learning. Next came the Confucian Analects, to emphasize the importance of the teachings of founder of the tradition. Mencius was placed third to reinforce his role in the interpretation of basic Confucian teachings. Last was the Doctrine of the Mean, whose subtlety and complexity could be viewed as a statement of the relation of the individual to the rest of the universe.

The question arises as to what makes these works scripture within the Confucian tradition. They are not individually called *ching*, or "classic," although two of them do come from one of the Five Classics. They include, however, the teachings of two of the founding figures of the tradition, Confucius and Mencius, who were not sages of antiquity. Is it appropriate to refer to the teachings of these men as scripture?

As the Confucian tradition evolved, the title of "sage" comes out of antiquity and begins to be applied to any appropriate individual. The Neo-Confucians in large part sought a form of personal education that would help one become a sage, not simply a form of learning that venerated the sages of antiquity. Thus, for the Neo-Confucians, Confucius and Mencius *were* sages, and they had heard the Way of *T'ien*. As such, their teachings contained the wisdom of the Way of Heaven and could be used by others who wanted to learn how to become sages, too.

Because they were seen as a source of knowledge about the Way of Heaven, the works could be viewed as foundational and authoritative for the Confucian tradition. The Four Books were given, in many ways, the same authority that had generally been attributed to the Five Classics alone. With this new authority, the Four Books became scripture, and they functioned as the scriptural basis for the development of the Neo-Confucian tradition.

Between the Five Classics and the Four Books, the Confucian tradition possesses a rich scriptural tradition. These works have continued to be used throughout the history of Confucianism, regardless of location. They are still seen as basic to contemporary practice.

4

Confucian Teachings

The ether of earth ascends,
the ether of heaven descends;
the Yin and Yang interact,
the forces of heaven and earth co-operate.
They are drummed on by thunder,
stirred by wind and rain,
kept in motion by the four seasons,
warmed by the sun and moon;
from all this the innumerable transformations arise.
This being so, music is the harmony of heaven and earth.

—Book of Rites 17:23

The Confucians who preserved and taught the ancient writings held the fundamental belief that these texts represented the sage rulers of antiquity. Tremendous authority was vested in these works as a record of the thoughts and deeds of the sages. The sages themselves were seen as individuals who had ruled through an understanding of the ultimate authority of the universe, *T'ien*, and thus could properly be called *T'ien-tzu*, or "Son of Heaven." They were said to rule under the authority of *T'ien ming*, the "Mandate of Heaven."

Confucius, on the basis of the teachings of the ancients, focused on the moral transformation of the individual and society as the remedy for the chaos of the time in which he lived. He looked to the rulers of his day to become true "Noble People" and as a result to become true rulers bearing the Mandate of Heaven and capable of uniting the empire by following Heaven's authority. Failing to find such a ruler, Confucius redirected his attention to teaching his disciples in the hope of transforming society through the creation of a widening circle of people who were educated according to the moral ways of the ancient rulers.

Confucius used the term *chün tzu*, noble person, as the central figure in his concept of moral transformation. Throughout the classical period of Confucianism and up to the beginnings of Neo-Confucianism, the *chün tzu* remained at the center of Confucian teachings. Following the advent of Neo-Confucianism, that center shifted from the *chün tzu* to the sage, or *sheng*, with the understanding that anyone could become a sage through learning and self-cultivation. Despite this shift, the understanding of humankind remained largely the same in terms of basic Confucian teachings. Even after Neo-Confucian thought added sophistication and new dimensions to the tradition, there remained a core of basic Confucian teachings.

CLASSICAL CONFUCIAN TEACHINGS

Classical Confucian ideas are the products of a group of early Confucians principally represented by Confucius, Mencius, and Hsün Tzu. Rather than considering their teachings separately, it is possible to talk in general terms about early Confucian thought, focusing on specific ideas largely shared by all Confucians. The most important of these teachings include *jen*, or "humaneness;" *i*, or "righteousness;" *li*, or "propriety/ritual;" and *hsing*, or "human nature." *Hsiao*, or "filial piety," is also a vital concept, one that is central for young people growing up in the Confucian tradition.

For the Confucian, these teachings may be said to characterize the ways of the sages of antiquity, who served as models for how to live. The teachings also came to characterize the idea of becoming a *chün tzu*, the ultimate goal of the moral cultivation of the individual. To understand the character of this noble person is to understand the nature of the traits that compose that moral character.

Humaneness

Jen, or humaneness, is probably the most commonly mentioned of Confucian virtues and the single most important teaching of Confucianism. The term, often depicted as a very general virtue in Confucian writings, has been translated in a wide variety of ways, in part reflecting the broad nature of the term, but also the complexity of trying to render the concept into another language. We can find *jen* translated as "benevolence," "compassion," "altruism," "goodness," "human-heartedness," "humanity," "love," "kindness," and "humaneness"—the last being the term that will be used here.

What does the Chinese character *jen* actually mean? It is composed of two parts, each a meaningful element. One part means "person," and the other part signifies the number "2." So, the word itself literally means something like "person 'two-ed'" or "person doubled." This definition suggests the relation of one person to another—and not just any relation, but the *proper* relation between two individuals. In this way, *jen* begins to refer to the moral relation of one to another, and thus, a sense of humaneness.

For all Confucians, *jen* is the most central teaching of the

THE CLASSIC OF FILIAL PIETY

The *Hsiao-ching*, or Classic of Filial Piety, became one of the most fundamental statements about the cardinal Confucian virtue of *hsiao*, or filial piety. Though not one of the original Five Classics, in later centuries it was added to an expanded canon of works called the Thirteen Classics. It is itself a product of the Han Dynasty, though tradition claims it was authored by a disciple of Confucius. There are a number of basic statements about the nature of filial piety that recur within this text, and because of this, it has been held in high respect through the centuries.

The passage that follows is representative of the way in which filial piety is described. There is little doubt about the nature of the relation between children and parents in this passage. With modernization came a strong rejection of this type of statement, though it is also apparent that the sentiment expressed is a deeply ingrained part of the Confucian heritage. At the heart of the notion of filial piety is the idea that one's body is a gift from one's parents and, for this reason, should be harmed as little as possible. In turn, the *Hsiao-ching* makes the virtue of filial piety the foundation for all other virtues:

> Our body, skin and hair are all received from our parents; we dare not injure them. This is the first priority in filial piety. To establish oneself in the world and practice the Way; to uphold one's good name for posterity and give glory to one's father and mother—this is the completion of filial piety. Thus filiality begins with service to parents, continues in service to the ruler, and ends with establishing oneself in the world (and becoming an exemplary person). . . . Filiality is the ordering principle of Heaven, the rightness of the Earth, and the norm of human conduct. This ordering of Heaven and Earth is what people should follow: illumined by the brightness of Heaven and benefited by the resources of Earth, all-under-Heaven are thus harmonized.*

* William Theodore de Bary and Irene Bloom, comp., *Sources of Chinese Tradition*, 2nd ed., vol. 1, New York: Columbia University Press, 1999, pp. 326–327.

tradition. It defines the basic relationship between people in a way that respects the moral integrity of the individual and his or her relation to others. Confucius described *jen* as the "single thread" that runs throughout his teachings. It is generally assumed to be the main characteristic of the noble person. For all later Confucians, it continues to play an essential role in defining the character of Confucian teachings and the ideal of either the noble person or the sage.

Can we describe *jen* in any more specific way? When asked about the "single thread" that runs through Confucius's teachings, a disciple commented that it may be described in several ways. In fact, two specific virtues are mentioned as ways to describe *jen*. These are the virtues of *chung*, or "conscientiousness," and *shu*, which means "sympathy" or "empathy." These words suggest a richer, deeper meaning for *jen*. On the one hand, *jen* means that a person demonstrates conscientiousness toward others, a sense of being concerned about people's well-being, and acts toward others with nurturing care and consideration. On the other hand, *jen* also has a level of sympathy, or empathy—the capacity to share in the feelings of others and to express one's own concern for any plight or misfortune that might befall them. This richer meaning is captured in part by the translations of *jen* as "humaneness" or "compassion," as opposed to simpler definitions like "goodness" or "love."

There is a famous passage in the Analects of Confucius that is taken as a description of the teaching of *jen*. It reads simply: "Do not do to others what you would not have them do to you." As has often been commented, it is essentially the Golden Rule of the Christian Bible. It says that an individual must consider the other person in all actions and not do something that he or she would not want done in return. This passage is a description of humaneness or goodness, and is a way of describing what should be the ideal moral relation between one person and another.

In describing this same virtue, Mencius says that it is

characteristic of human beings, whose basic nature is goodness, not to be able to bear to see the suffering of another person. This does not mean that some people are not capable of hurting others. Rather, it suggests that human nature has the ability to express goodness and, though it can be turned to evil, goodness is the true state of human nature, a goodness defined in terms of the virtue of *jen*.

It is difficult to overestimate the significance of this virtue or teaching to the Confucian tradition as a whole. In fact, one can say that across the centuries of the history of Confucianism, the teaching of *jen* would be the one consistently defining characteristic of the tradition. Whatever century, whatever school of thought, whatever individual Confucian, *jen* has always played a central part.

Righteousness
I is usually translated as "righteousness" (though it can also be translated as something like "conscience"). It means being able to distinguish between right and wrong; it is almost an inner judge within an individual. In this sense, the word *conscience* applies very well to the idea of *I*. To say that someone has a conscience is to say that he or she will act on the basis of an inner sense of right and wrong. This distinction between right and wrong does not necessarily follow popular opinion alone. In fact, in most cases when someone is described as acting based on conscience, it means that he or she has made decisions based on a higher sense of right and wrong. In other words, he or she has not gone along with the majority point of view, because that point of view did not correspond with a higher sense of what was right, according to that individual's beliefs in a particular situation.

When Confucians discuss righteousness or conscience, they often describe it by explaining what it is *not*. In this case, righteousness or conscience is said to be the opposite of *li*, or "profit," and *yung*, "utility." Profit and utility describe two reasons that a person might consider doing something.

Someone might say, for example, if I take a certain action, I will profit; or, he might say that the action will be useful to him, or to family or friends. From the Confucian point of view, these are the wrong motivations to use when judging whether an action should be carried out. The sole concern from the Confucian point of view is whether the action is ultimately right or wrong—that is, whether it is morally right or wrong in and of itself, regardless of possible consequences, good or bad. This question of moral right or wrong takes precedence over any potential thought of how useful or profitable something might be to the individual, or to society, for that matter.

This teaching proved difficult for Confucius and his followers. They were, after all, attempting to convince the rulers of their day to adopt their beliefs. As Confucius and his followers often discovered, the only real point of interest for any ruler of the day was the degree to which Confucian teachings would prove useful to his particular state in this period of terrible civil strife and great contention between states for power. Teachings that stressed doing only what was morally right with no thought of utility or profit were of little interest to political leaders. For this reason, the Confucians met with little success in their attempts to turn the rulers of their day toward their line of thought.

The concept of *I*, even after Confucianism had begun to change over the years, at times produced very grave difficulties for Confucians. Problems arose especially when Confucians served in high governmental positions, giving advice to emperors. Such situations sometimes produced the classic example of a battle of wills: The emperor may want to launch a military campaign to seize more territory. He sees that these actions will bring him great profit and will be highly useful, considering the additional resources that will be added to the realm. The Confucian minister is asked for his advice. Under some circumstances, the Confucian minister might be in complete agreement with the emperor's plan, if he believes there is some specific justification for military action. However, in this particular case, he realizes that the emperor's decision rests solely on a desire for profit, and finds that there are no moral grounds to support the cause. His decision is that the proposed action is morally unjustifiable and he requests that the emperor desist in his plans.

From the Confucian point of view, no other decision is possible. It is a decision based on what is morally right. In some cases, the emperor might have accepted such advice; in other cases, though, the Confucian minister might be punished—a punishment that resulted from taking a moral stand in the face of a potentially immoral act. To stick by a decision based on a moral determination, no matter what the consequences, is part of the nature of this teaching of *I*. A Confucian minister of state did not relinquish a moral conviction, regardless of the fact that his action might lead to demotion, banishment, imprisonment, torture, or even execution. Moral right from the Confucian perspective was more important than even one's own life. The history of Confucianism is filled with individuals who became martyrs to the cause of *I*.

Rites or Propriety

Li, translated as "rites" or "propriety," is a teaching found throughout the writings of the ancient sages, particularly the several writings that make up the Classic or Book of Rites. Much of the world of the sage rulers represented in the Chinese Classics is dominated by ritual performance. There are rituals for virtually every occasion and each is seen as significant in terms of the role of the sage ruler and his relation to the authority of *T'ien*. Such ritual reflected the order and structure that dominated not only the individual life of the sage ruler, but the larger society over which he ruled. In turn, it was believed that this order and structure was a mirror image of the order and structure that existed in Heaven itself, as the ruling authority over the entire universe.

Ritual, then, was not simply a casual performance of ceremonies. Instead, it was seen as directly connected to the moral order of the cosmos. At one level, ritual was a way for the individual to show respect to Heaven itself for the organization of all things. At another level, the ritual was itself the way in which moral order was maintained.

The Confucians, as the transmitters of the ancient writings, found a particular importance in preserving the ritual culture that represented China at the time of the sage rulers. As a result, there is much attention paid in Confucian writings to the importance of the ancient rituals. Beginning with the thoughts of Confucius himself, there are a number of passages that discuss the preservation of ritual and the importance of the proper performance of such rites. There are passages, for example, where Confucius is asked to spare the expenditures of ritual by limiting the number of items sacrificed or to lessen the suffering of sacrificed animals by reducing the number of animals included. In each case, Confucius responds by reinforcing the importance of performing the ritual fully and accurately, because he sees such acts not only as something mandated by the sage rulers of antiquity, but also as a symbol of the broader moral order of the universe. The accuracy of the ritual was important, and the Confucians took responsibility for the preservation of the exact form of ancient rituals.

In terms of ritual, Confucius served as both a transmitter and a creator. He emphasized not just the details of ancient rites, but also a critically important element of Confucian understanding of ritual. One can imagine that the ancient culture the Confucians sought to preserve might very well have seen the most important element in ritual as its accuracy and, in fact, might have concluded that any mistake in a ritual performance rendered the act ineffective. From the Confucian perspective, accurate performance was important, but not the most critical element. In a passage in the Analects, Confucius laments that ritual has become nothing more than a mere performance, and he protests this. If the ceremony is performed with accuracy in all its details, what is missing, in Confucius's opinion? The answer is inner feeling. In fact, it is inner feeling that is the key to ritual.

A person performs ritual not for its own sake, but in order to enter into a special relationship with the object of the ritual. For the ruler, or Son of Heaven, the object is Heaven; for the individual, it may be the family, ancestors, or a variety of other possibilities. The point, of course, is that ritual is a symbol of the moral relations that tie all people and the entire world together. To experience the feelings of the ritual is to understand the larger moral implications of ritual performance. Without this broader understanding, there is nothing to the ritual but a physical performance. Although for some, this kind of performance might be quite adequate and efficacious, for a Confucian, it is the inner feelings—not the act of the ritual itself—that represent the real meaning.

This extended sense of inner feelings provides a broadened sense of the meaning of ritual for the Confucian. The term *li* originally meant "ritual," "rite," or even "sacrifice." The Chinese character for the word was a pictogram of a sacrificial vessel being presented to a spirit. The term can be used, however, in a very broad context, one that falls outside of the strict use of the term *ritual* itself. For example, it can be said that one acts in a fashion of *li*, ritual, toward his or her elders. That does not mean he or she performs constant rituals for the benefit of elders. Rather, it means that the person behaves with a ritual attitude. But what does it mean to act with a ritual attitude? It means that one acts with propriety or an attitude of deference toward others.

Again, one does not normally think of a connection between the terms *ritual* and *propriety*. In a very real sense, however, propriety is, by definition, acting ritually. This connection is, for the Confucian, a demonstration of the degree to which all behavior may be considered ritual behavior because it is done out of deference to the moral authority of sage rulers and the ultimate authority of Heaven. It is showing deference to the moral structure of the world in which we live.

Human Nature and Learning

With the ideal of the noble person, Confucians placed major significance on the ability of each individual to learn to become moral. Self-cultivation was aimed at the development of the kind of teachings described: humaneness, righteousness, and ritual and propriety. The question that arose early in the Confucian tradition was whether such qualities were inherent in the individual or were to be acquired from outside. The Confucians believed that the models for these teachings were the sages of antiquity; no one doubted the sages' ability to embody these virtues in their highest form. The question, of course, was whether all people shared the same nature as the sages.

Confucius himself did not address the question of human nature. He left that issue to be debated by the major teachers who followed him. Essentially, two positions developed on the question, one from Mencius and one from Hsün Tzu. It is important to remember that in the early days of Confucianism, Hsün Tzu was the most prominent interpreter of Confucius. Mencius was virtually unknown to his own generation, even though later, after the advent of Neo-Confucianism, he was recognized as the orthodox interpreter of Confucius.

On the question of human nature, Mencius and Hsün Tzu appear to have had very different interpretations. For Mencius, human nature was originally good. This does not mean that there are not evil people, but Mencius saw evil as a violation of the original good. In this respect, everyone has the same nature as the sages of antiquity, although the natures of the sages were fully realized, whereas ordinary people had to make great efforts to realize their own capacity to be a sage. Mencius defines this human nature in terms of *jen, I, li,* and *chih,* or "wisdom." Mencius said that human responsibility lies with developing the inner moral nature with which each person is born. Learning, though arduous, was essentially focused on manifesting more fully what was already inherent within human nature.

For Hsün Tzu, by contrast, human nature was deficient without thorough learning and education. He even suggested that human nature in the raw was evil. (Hsün Tzu was the only Confucian philosopher to take this position.) Although this suggestion was never taken very seriously in the tradition, Hsün Tzu does represent a major trend within Confucian thought. This trend believed that human nature was in need of diligent effort in education under the very strict models of the sages of antiquity. Though Mencius came to dominate Confucian thought, Hsün Tzu played a critical role in emphasizing the Confucian tradition's belief in the importance of education in the process of the transformation of a person into a moral individual. It is a matter of degree as to how much moral quality the individual begins with, but there is a steady tradition of emphasis on the absolute necessity of learning to create the moral person, the noble person, envisioned by Confucius with the full embodiment of the virtues of humaneness, righteousness, and ritual or propriety and wisdom, as a reflection of the moral character of the sages of antiquity and ultimately heaven itself. It rested with the Neo-Confucians to bring philosophical sophistication to these teachings as well as the proximity of the sage as a model to emulate.

NEO-CONFUCIAN TEACHINGS

What makes Neo-Confucianism different from traditional Confucianism is its more philosophical orientation and the degree to which it is a response to both Buddhism and Taoism. Neo-Confucianism entertains questions about what human nature is like and what its relation is to the rest of the universe at a far more sophisticated level than earlier Confucian teachings did. The various schools of Neo-Confucianism have very different understandings of human nature and the universe, a universe now understood in terms of a philosophical system rather than the simple ethical teachings of the Confucian predecessors. It is not that the ethical teachings are put aside, but rather that they are brought into a more elaborate system of ideas, including theories about the origins of the cosmos.

Neo-Confucianism is also different from earlier Confucianism because it represents a very conscious response to Buddhism and Taoism, one that is both negative and positive. On the one hand, Neo-Confucianism originally grew as an attempt to counter what were seen as the otherworldly characteristics of Buddhism and Taoism. To the Confucians, humankind's concern should be with real problems in the world, not the seeking of a spiritual release from the world itself. On the other hand, the Confucians recognized that both Buddhism and Taoism provided a model for religious life and could play a valuable role in establishing guidelines for a more spiritual life within Confucianism. As a result, the spiritual or religious life in Neo-Confucianism became much more significant than it had been in earlier Confucianism.

A basic core of teachings characterizes the Neo-Confucian movement, which stretches across a wide range of time and cultural settings and represents a broad variety of individuals. Basic Confucian values and teachings were reaffirmed, including the cultivation of sagehood as a religious goal and the need to take moral action in the world. Neo-Confucians felt the need to reemphasize the old teachings because many of these ideas seemed to have fallen into eclipse, particularly during the years after the end of the Han Dynasty and into the T'ang Dynasty, when the expansion of Buddhism and Taoism reached its height. It was the Neo-Confucians who established Mencius as the interpreter of Confucius, and, with this move, they were able to draw attention to the theory of the goodness of human nature as well as the foundation of teaching in terms of the basic virtues of Confucianism— humaneness, righteousness, ritual, and propriety.

The traditional Confucian ideal of the *chün tzu*, or noble

KAIBARA EKKEN'S INSTRUCTIONS FOR CHILDREN

One of the great Neo-Confucian teachers in Japan, Kaibara Ekken (1630–1714), was responsible for the creation of a set of fundamental Confucian teachings for children. These teachings are based on a Confucian view of the interrelations between all people and things in the universe. He told children that just as we express our love toward our parents, who have given us life, we should also express our love toward Heaven, which is the source of all life. These ideas are grounded in the teaching of *jen* ("humaneness"), or, as it is translated here, "benevolence." *Nature* refers to the world as we know it, but at the same time, it is also the nature of Heaven, because from the Neo-Confucian point of view, all things ultimately hold the moral nature of Heaven within them.

> To persist in the service of Heaven means that everyone who is a man should be mindful of the fact that morning and evening he is in the presence of heaven, and not far removed from it; that he should fear and reverence the way of heaven and not be unmindful of it. . . . [F]ollowing the way of Heaven, he should be humble and not arrogant toward others, control his desires and not be indulgent of his passions, cherish a profound love for all mankind born of nature's great love, and not abuse or mistreat them. Nor should he waste, just to gratify his personal desires, the five grains and other bounties which nature has provided for the sake of the people. Secondly, no living creatures such as birds, beasts, insects, and fish should be killed wantonly. Not even grass and trees should be cut down out of season. All these are objects of nature's love, having been brought forth by her and nurtured by her. To cherish them and keep them is therefore the way to serve nature in accordance with the great heart of nature. Among human obligations there is first the duty to love our relatives, then to show sympathy for all other human beings, and then not to mistreat birds and beasts or any other living things. That is the proper order for the practice of benevolence in accordance with the great heart of nature.*

* Ryusaku Tsunoda, William Theodore de Bary, and Donde Keene, eds., *Sources of Japanese Tradition*, vol. 1, New York: Columbia University Press, 1964, p. 368.

person, was also transformed for the Neo-Confucians to the *sheng*, or sage. With the acceptance of Mencius as the orthodox interpreter of Confucius, the ideal of the sage moved out of antiquity and became a goal for every individual. Mencius had said that anyone could become a sage, and the Neo-Confucians took him seriously. Mencius did not mean that the goal of sagehood was easily accessible for most people. In fact, for most people, it remained largely unapproachable. Now, however, it was believed to be possible and came to be considered the direct object of learning and self-cultivation.

We have described the *Li hsüeh*, or School of Principle, and the *Hsin hsüeh*, or School of Mind, the two major schools of Neo-Confucianism. These divisions differed in their understanding of the self-cultivation process required to achieve sagehood because of subtle differences in their philosophical understanding of human nature. They were united, however, in their conviction that the individual needed to seek moral transformation, to work toward the goal of sagehood. Even the *shih hsüeh*, School of Practical Learning, which sought to turn away from the more philosophical teachings of the School of Principle and the School of Mind, did not reject the goal of sagehood. It defined sagehood in terms of the basic moral teachings of early Confucianism, but it retained that ideal state as the aim Confucians hoped to reach.

For all Neo-Confucians, then, sagehood was the goal of religious life. This religious life, in turn, was measured in terms of the Confucian's ability not to renounce the world as some believed the Buddhists and Taoists advocated, but to commit to the moral transformation of the world.

The end result of these concepts was that the Neo-Confucians were committed to taking moral action in the world. They saw in early Confucianism a tradition that focused on moral action and they sought to recapture this tone of the early teachings. Even as they became more interested in philosophical discussion and the cultivation of sagehood, they did not abandon the emphasis on the need to establish an agenda of moral prerogatives for acting in the world. They saw their own reestablishment of Confucianism as a way of embracing this fundamental idea—to act and to transform the world through the power of the moral teachings of the sages of antiquity and through their own learning and self-cultivation.

5

A Visit to the Confucian Temple

When the Master entered the great temple
he asked about everything. Someone said,
"Who will say that this son of the man
Zhou [Confucius's father] knows about ritual?
When he enters the great temple,
he asks about everything." The Master
heard of it and said, "This is the ritual."

—Analects 3:15

O great teacher thy virtue surpasses that of a thousand sages
And thy way excels that of a hundred kings.
Rivaling the sun and the moon,
Thy light shines forever.
Truly there is none
Like thee among us.

This verse is part of a prayer to Confucius. It represents the establishment of the Confucian tradition in an institutional form, what became known as the Confucian Temple. The prayer itself was something that would be used in the major ritual activity of the Confucian Temple, a twice-yearly sacrifice to Confucius, held in the spring and fall of each year. The ceremony was called the *shih-tien* ceremony, or Twice Yearly Confucian Ceremony. This activity seems to have developed from a ritual originally conducted to commemorate Confucius, probably within a few years of his death in 479 B.C. It continued over the centuries, ending formally in the early part of the twentieth century with the demise of the Confucian Temple as an institution. The Temple and the Twice Yearly Confucian Ceremony developed in each of the cultures that adopted Confucianism under the Chinese sphere of influence.

A BRIEF HISTORY OF THE CONFUCIAN
TEMPLE AND CONFUCIAN CEREMONY

The beginnings of the Confucian Temple appear to be rooted in Chinese religious beliefs about celebrating and remembering ancestors. Every Chinese family venerates its ancestors with the belief that the ancestors' continued happiness is linked to the family's devotion to their memory and needs. Each home has an ancestral altar, shrine, or hall, and family members conduct rituals and make offerings that are thought to benefit their ancestors in the other world. The K'ung family, Confucius's family, was no different. The K'ung family home in Ch'ü-fu had an ancestral hall where ancestors were venerated. After his death, Confucius became one of those ancestors.

As Confucius's reputation grew, the ancestral hall of the K'ung family was visited by more people than just members of the K'ung family. The origins of the Confucian Temple as an institution lay in the ritual veneration of Confucius by individuals not associated with the family. Over time, some of those who came to show respect for Confucius were people of high stature, and their actions helped the K'ung ancestral hall to grow. For example, Emperor Kao Tsu of the Former Han Dynasty (c. 206 B.C.–A.D. 8) stopped at the K'ung family ancestral hall and offered a sacrifice to Confucius in 195 B.C. The Latter Han Dynasty (c. A.D. 25–220) records visits by at least three emperors, each of whom offered a sacrifice to Confucius. The particular sacrifice that was offered on these occasions was the *t'ai-lao*, or Great Offering, a ritual that was performed under only the most special of circumstances. A sacrifice of this magnitude, done by an emperor, served to indicate the esteem in which Confucius was beginning to be held.

Even with the highly prestigious Great Offering being presented to Confucius by emperors, such ceremonies were technically still private events held at a family's ancestral hall; they were not an official ritual. During the T'ang Dynasty, however, a separate institution, known as the Confucian Temple, began to grow at the state level. The T'ang Emperor Kao Tsu ordered a temple for Confucius and the Duke of Chou to be built in the capital in A.D. 619. The building soon became a temple devoted entirely to Confucius. By 630, Emperor T'ai Tsung ordered that temples devoted to Confucius be built in provincial capitals throughout the country. By this time, other figures were being honored in the main Temple, too. It included not just Confucius, but a number of his disciples and other important Confucians throughout history. Over the centuries, new figures would be added to the Temple and, in some cases, taken away.

With a very strong link between Confucianism and the state through most of Confucian history, the Confucian Temple became a major center for state ceremony. Thus, the Great Offering continued to remain the principal means of offering sacrifice at Confucian temples. Ceremony at the Confucian Temple reflected in historic periods the influence and power of the state and the link that the state saw between its own power and the teachings of Confucius. State ideology and Confucian teachings were seen as one and the same. Through this identification, Confucianism became the state's official ideology.

As the Confucian Temple developed, it was known by a number of different names, including *hsien sheng miao* (Temple of the Sage of Antiquity), *wen miao* (Temple of Culture), *K'ung tzu miao* (Temple of Confucius), and *Wen hsüan wang miao* (Temple of the Comprehensive King).

TOURING A CONFUCIAN TEMPLE

In general design and layout, the Confucian Temple is very similar to temple complexes found across China and other Asian cultures under China's historic influence. The Confucian Temple complex in particular shares a number of features with imperial architectural structures, including its geographical orientation as well as various decorative symbols associated with imperial authority. In the imperial model, buildings are oriented on a north-south axis. The emperor was the only person permitted to face south. All other people had to face north when in audience with the emperor. To symbolize his position and power, the emperor was likened to the pole star. Like the pole star, he remained motionless while all others moved around him. His direction was north and all others were south of him. The Confucian Temple, too, was built on a north-south axis, with the position of greatest honor held by Confucius and his ancestors, at the north of the Temple complex.

Approaching a Confucian Temple, one enters the compound at the southernmost point of its north-south axis. The route to the entrance will frequently have a series of gates under which one must pass, each with some reference to Confucius or the Confucian Temple painted, engraved, or carved upon it. For example, one might say, *chin-sheng yü-chen* ("Metal Begins, Jade Closes"), a reference to part of the Twice Yearly Confucian

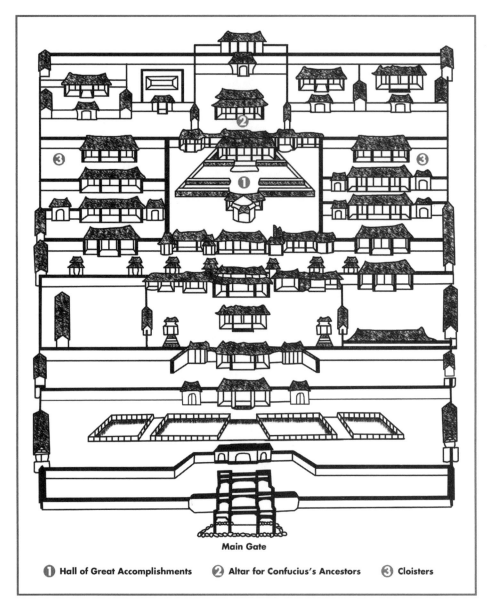

Main Gate

① Hall of Great Accomplishments   ② Altar for Confucius's Ancestors   ③ Cloisters

The many Confucian temples that were built throughout Asia tended to follow the same basic plan, similar to the one seen here. Visitors entered the compound through gates (bottom) and progressed past the various buildings and statues erected to honor Confucius and others revered within the tradition.

Ceremony in which bronze bells open the ceremony and jade chimes close it. Another might say *t'ai-ho yuan-ch'i* ("Primordial Vitality of the Supreme Harmony"), a reference to Confucius from a phrase found in one of the Five Classics.

Once inside the Temple complex, the visitor faces the main building of the Temple directly to the north. The path to the building is straight and is lined with several statues of famous Confucians, such as Confucius's disciple Yen Hui and the Classical Confucian Mencius. The path also boasts juniper and ginkgo trees, both of which have long been associated with Confucianism.

The building itself is called the *ta-ch'eng tien*, or "Hall of Great Accomplishments." It contains the main altar to Confucius, located at the northernmost point of the Temple. The structure is essentially identical to an imperial audience hall, where the emperor would receive guests from his position at the northern edge of the building. To the sides of the main altar are several smaller altars, some dedicated to those referred to as "Worthies," others dedicated to those called "Philosophers." (The Temple had various ranks; people were chosen based on their importance as Confucians.) Those honored by the side altars have been subject to change; individuals have been added and removed over the years. There is a terrace in front of the building that is used during the Twice Yearly Confucian Ceremony to house the traditional orchestra that performs during the ritual.

On the same north-south axis, there is one building that—surprisingly—sits north of the main altar dedicated to Confucius, suggesting greater prestige than that of Confucius himself. This is the building that contains an altar to commemorate the five generations of Confucian ancestors. It recognizes the founder of Confucius's family as well as Confucius's own father. Confucius's ancestors are given the highest stature in the veneration of Confucius.

Outside and to the sides of the main building are more buildings, devoted to additional Confucians who made noteworthy accomplishments. These buildings, laid out symmetrically on either side of the main hall, are called the Cloisters. They house representations of those referred to as "Former Worthies" and "Former Confucians." These figures, too, can be added to or removed over time. Such changes seem to depend in large part on how an individual's contribution to an important aspect of the Confucian tradition is assessed at a given time. Because Confucianism's emphasis has changed across centuries, those who are considered most notable have changed as well.

Several other features of the Temple deserve mention. In the Confucian Temple, there will be a number of erect stone tablets, usually located toward the front of the complex. These tablets, called steles, commemorate visits to the Temple by famous individuals, usually public officials. They stand many feet tall and contain verses and thoughts carved in stone to capture the feelings of an important dignitary on his visit to the Temple. There is also a small stone oven in the Temple complex. It is used during the Twice Yearly Confucian Ceremony to ritually burn the official address used during the ritual.

CONFUCIAN SYMBOLS AND IMPERIAL SYMBOLS

A close-up look at the Confucian Temple buildings and their architecture reveals a number of symbols that are important to the understanding of Confucianism. Because of the close relation that developed between Confucianism and the Chinese state, many of these symbols were originally associated with imperial authority. As Confucianism became the state ideology, its temple institution reflected the state institutions it represented. Typically, symbols used in the Confucian Temple are also seen in historic imperial buildings, such as the Forbidden City, the historic imperial residence in Beijing.

The *ta-ch'eng tien*, or Hall of Great Accomplishments, comprises a series of symbols that portray imperial authority. The columns in front of the building are carved with dragons. Placed in the middle of the steps leading to the terrace of the building is a large stone relief carving of a dragon. The central ceiling ornament is also a dragon. Dragons are a symbol of power and have long been associated with imperial authority.

Given the role of Confucianism within the state, it is not surprising that they are also found in the Confucian Temple. Dragons are often shown with different numbers of claws. Those associated with imperial authority always have five claws, and so do those found in the Confucian Temple. The dragons are frequently depicted holding a sacred pearl, another symbol of imperial authority.

The phoenix is another image displayed in the main hall. This bird has a long association with imperial authority. Roof ornaments show a variety of extraordinary beasts, including the unicorn, yet another image associated with imperial authority. One story says that when an emperor visited the Confucian Temple, some of these imperial symbols would be covered up so as not to diminish the power and authority of the visiting ruler. Although the state benefited by being able to describe itself as Confucian, certainly Confucianism was established in its importance through its use of the symbols that represented the greatest authority of the land.

CONFUCIAN ICONOGRAPHY

Iconography is the way in which a figure is shown or displayed, whether in painting, sculpture, stone carving, or any other art form, either representational or symbolic. Confucius has been depicted by several different images, including the symbols just discussed. He may be portrayed as a loyal minister of state, a retiring and gentle teacher and scholar, or even as a ruler himself. In each of these roles, his clothing and his implements contain the symbols associated with these positions. For example, as ruler, he is shown at the head of his disciples, wearing imperial attire and a crown. As minister of state, he wears official courtly dress and carries a tablet, a symbol of the loyal minister recording the words of his ruler. As a teacher, he is shown in a retiring and gentle style. His clothing is often old and even worn. At times, he will carry a writing brush to symbolize his role as scholar and teacher.

For most of the institution's history, no visual representation of Confucius or his disciples was allowed within the Confucian Temple. Prohibitions against visual representation were intended primarily to differentiate Confucianism from other religions in which visual images of a whole range of supernatural beings were common. Instead, Confucius and his disciples were represented in the same way that ancestors are represented in a family's ancestral hall—with a *shen wei*, or ancestral tablet. A person's title or name was placed on the tablet, but apart from that, there was no further representation. Though many different titles have been used for Confucius across the centuries, one of the most commonly used is *Ta-ch'eng chih-sheng K'ung-Tzu hsien-shih*, or "Teacher of Antiquity, Confucius, of Greatest Accomplishment and Highest Sageliness."

WITNESSING A CONFUCIAN CEREMONY

The major ceremony associated with Confucianism, *shih-tien*, the Twice Yearly Confucian Ceremony, brings ritual and liturgical life to the Confucian Temple. Its origins are closely associated with the adaptation of state ceremony and sacrifice to the developing tradition of venerating Confucius, his disciples, and his teachings.

In traditional state sacrifice there were three levels. The highest level was reserved for sacrifices to Heaven, Earth, and Confucius. In terms of the actual sacrifice made to each of these sources of authority, there was very little difference. Emperor Han Kao Tsu began the tradition of sacrifice to Confucius. His sacrifice was the *t'ai-lao*, or the Great Offering. This highest form of sacrifice included the meat of three animals—pig, ox, and sheep. It was the same offering conducted to honor Heaven and Earth. Some details of the Great Offering have changed over time, and variations have often been allowed, particularly in different cultural settings. As the Confucian Temple and the Twice Yearly Confucian Ceremony developed, however, the sacrifice to Confucius remained the highest level of ceremony attainable.

The Twice Yearly Confucian Ceremony is a sacrifice offered to Confucius, along with the various categories of Confucians represented in the Confucian Temple, including Worthies, Philosophers, Former Worthies, and Former Confucians. The ceremony presented three separate offerings, and it was organized around the introduction and conclusion of each of these. The entire ceremony has six stages, each defined by the presentation of a liturgical verse sung by the master celebrant, a distinguished Confucian.

The first stage, called Radiant Peace, begins the ceremony. It welcomes the arrival of the spirit of Confucius at the ceremony. All participants are in place—musicians, celebrants, ritual attendants, and dancers. The orchestra plays and the celebrant sings a set liturgical verse to welcome the spirit. Prostrations are made to Confucius and the other Confucians honored in the Temple. Music accompanies each portion of the unfolding ceremony.

The second stage, Manifested Peace, is accompanied by the orchestra and singing. It represents the first of three sacrificial offerings that make up the ceremony. Like the first stage, it begins with a liturgical verse sung by the celebrant. The celebrant then approaches the altar and makes the offering. The first offering usually consists of grain, silk, and fruit. Returning to his place, the celebrant then makes triple prostrations by kneeling and bowing.

The third stage, Regulated Peace, begins with another liturgical verse sung by the celebrant. At this point, there is a second offering, an animal sacrifice. The animals, already cooked and prepared, are presented by the celebrant, who again makes triple prostrations. At this stage, there is the formal presentation of a Ritual Address, a short speech directed toward Confucius, which is read by the chief celebrant. It praises Confucius in similar fashion to the liturgical verses themselves, admiring his incomparable wisdom and the virtue of his teachings. The Ritual Address, too, is followed by triple prostrations. Following the address, formal dances may be performed. These are referred to as the Civil Dance and the Military Dance.

The fourth stage, Ordered Peace, begins with yet another liturgical verse sung by the celebrant. At this point in the ceremony, the third and final offering is presented. It is an offering of wine. Only at this stage does the celebrant actually partake of the offerings. This is considered the most significant moment of the ritual, as the spirit and the human consume the offerings together.

The fifth stage, Beauteous Peace, begins as each of other stages does, with the singing of a liturgical verse by the celebrant. This stage focuses simply upon the ritual removal of the offerings and the ritual vessels as part of the conclusion of the ceremony.

The sixth stage, Virtuous Peace, also has a liturgical verse that is sung, which includes a final passage such as:

> *To the grand hall of learning,*
> *Scholars from the four quarters of the horizon*
> *Come to show respect.*
> *Reverently they perform the ceremonies of the sacrifice,*
> *With all solemn show required of the ritual.*
> *The spirit having enjoyed the fragrant odors of the gifts*
> *Returns to its place.*
> *The presentation of the offerings is finished.*
> *All who have shared in the ceremony enjoy great variety of happiness.*

It is believed that, at this stage of the ceremony, the spirit leaves and returns to its own realm. As a final act, the Ritual Address is then burned, symbolizing its transfer to the realm of the spirits. With this burning, the ceremony comes to a formal end.

THE TEMPLE AS A RELIGIOUS INSTITUTION

The existence of the Confucian Temple, with its traditions of sacrifice, prayer, and ceremony raises fundamental questions about Confucianism as a religious tradition. One might ask, if the Confucian Temple is to be taken seriously, then why has there ever been a question about whether Confucianism is religious? After all, it offers prayers and sacrifices to its founder. It performs the highest level of sacrifice to Confucius, regarding him as an uncrowned emperor more august than all the rulers of history. He is presented as a cultic figure of god-like proportions. Is this not the stuff of religion?

Before answering this, it is important to remember the grounds upon which some have argued that Confucianism is not a religion. Confucius said that one must keep the spirits at a distance, and he indicated that he had no knowledge of life after death. In other words, he appeared to consider the supernatural and the miraculous irrelevant. In place of such otherworldly concerns was an emphasis on moral learning to create a world of peace and order here on Earth, a world that conformed to the Way of *T'ien.* Did this message change after Confucius's death? We know that it did not, because the form of Confucianism that became dominant reaffirmed and reinforced the priorities of original Confucian teachings.

How, then, should the Confucian Temple be explained? What is its role within the Confucian tradition? First, the Confucian Temple and its ritual ceremony originated with religious practices associated with the state. The Great Offering at the state level was believed to attract spirits, and it was believed that the spirits actually partook of the sacrifice, enjoying the offering and then sending blessings as a reward to the celebrants. From the outset, the Confucians had a very different interpretation of the meaning and role of ritual. To them, ritual was a symbol of the order of the universe, a critical element in the structure of the Way of Heaven. To perform ritual was to conform to Heaven's Way. The fact that such ritual might be focused on the realm of spirits was secondary to the importance of ritual itself. Thus, Confucius says that people should perform sacrifice *as if* the spirits were there. Their actual presence is largely unimportant and is secondary at best to the true purpose of ritual, to conform to the order of the universe. Does this mean that Confucian ceremony is, therefore, not religious? Not at all. However, it is religious not because it accepts the existence of the supernatural as most other faiths do, but because it views the performance of ritual as a way of conforming to the Way of Heaven.

6

Growing up Confucian

Among those who are filial toward their
parents and fraternal toward their brothers,
those who are inclined to offend against
their superiors are few indeed. . . . Being filial
and fraternal—is this not the root of humaneness?

—Analects 1:2

To grow up Confucian meant in large part to be raised with a set of values rooted in the Confucian tradition, to be educated about the network of relationships that make up the family, society, the world, and Heaven itself. Virtually every aspect of one's life was tied in to these values. These complex relationships included both the living and the dead, as well as those both higher and lower in society. The overarching principle was to see these relationships as the basis for moral interactions between individuals, between the individual and society, between society and the ruler, and, ultimately, between the ruler and *T'ien*, the moral absolute of the universe.

Growing up Confucian, one was slowly introduced to this set of relationships. The family, society, the world, and the cosmos beyond were represented as a hierarchy in which the individual was expected to learn his or her own place and to act in ways that were suitable to that position. A Confucian was taught to behave in a manner that demonstrated moral responsibility and obligation irrespective of the setting.

The starting point for all such learning was the family itself, the single most important set of relations to help a person understand both oneself and one's relation to others. Confucianism was built upon the centrality of the family; therefore, growing up Confucian meant first and foremost developing an understanding of one's relation with the family.

Confucianism accepted that the family was composed of both the living and dead. Family members had an obligation to care for departed ancestors through ritual and sacrifice, to make sure their needs were provided for in the next world. Introduced to this tradition as a child, Confucians discovered a sense of caring and love among all family members, coupled with an understanding of the mutual responsibilities that existed among relatives. All these relationships were ultimately seen as part of the moral universe.

The overarching Confucian worldview suggested that the focus of life was on the individual's effort to become a moral person. Confucian teachings stressed the ways of the ancient sage rulers as guide for creating a moral society. Such a society depended, in the Confucian mind, on the singular importance of each individual's quest to become a moral person. By becoming moral, it was believed that each person would then behave in moral ways in regard to those around him or her. If everyone learned to become moral, and thus acted in a moral way toward others, society as a whole would become moral. This general perspective on the importance of learning to be moral applied to everyone in society, from the common person up to the ruler himself.

Though focused upon the importance of individual learning, Confucians gave the ruler a critical role to play in the creation of a moral society. Unlike the ordinary person, the ruler served as a model for the entire realm. That meant it was even more important for the ruler to develop his moral nature and behave in moral ways. By doing so, he would be able to understand the Way of *T'ien*. The ruler was called the Son of Heaven, a title that suggested the ruler's importance in carrying out the Mandate of Heaven, the moral ordering of the world. If the ruler exercised his role as Son of Heaven, each person under his dominion, however far removed, would have a model of what constituted the moral nature and what the ultimate relation of humankind to heaven should be.

THE GREAT LEARNING—A MODEL FOR MATURATION
The model for the Confucian was clear from the earliest phase of the tradition. All importance lay with the learning, education, and self-cultivation necessary to become a fully moral person. Such learning always began with the individual and worked outward toward others. The steps of learning represented in the work *Ta hsüeh*, one of the Four Books, is illustrative of this emphasis. Of the eight steps of learning discussed in the text, five focus on the individual, rather than on society or the world. Only after a person has fully developed his or her own moral nature may he or she then turn outward to the broader base of learning by handling relations with the family and society and ultimately bringing

INSTRUCTIONS FOR CHILDREN

The following is a well-known example of school guidelines for the conduct of children. This particular set of rules, a product of disciples of the twelfth-century Neo-Confucian Chu Hsi, establishes a stringent code of behavior, emphasizing the seriousness of the educational process.

1. Learning the rites: To be (truly) human, one must know the Way and its principles and the different ritual prescriptions. At home one must serve parents; at the academy one must serve his teacher. They are entitled to equal respect and compliance. Follow their instructions. Listen to what they say; do what they prescribe. Do not be lazy, careless, or presumptuous.

2. Learning to sit: Settle yourself and sit straight; control your hands and feet; do not sit cross-legged or lean on anything; do not lie back or lean down.

3. Learning to walk: Hold your arms in and walk slowly; do not swing your arms or jump about.

4. Learning to stand: Fold your hands and straighten your body; do not lean to one side or slouch over.

5. Learning to speak: Be plain and honest in your speech; do not lie or boast; speak softly and circumspectly; do not yell or shout.

6. Learning to bow (in salute): Lower the head and bend at the waist; speak without gesticulating; do not be flippant or rude.

7. Learning to recite: Look at the characters with undivided attention; read slowly, short passages at a time; clearly distinguish, character by character; do not look at anything else or let your hands fiddle with anything.

8. Learning to write: Grasp the brush with firm intent; the characters must be balanced, regular, and perfectly clear; there must be no carelessness or messiness.

* William Theodore de Bary and Irene Bloom, comp., *Sources of Chinese Tradition*, 2nd ed., vol. 1, New York: Columbia University Press, 1999, p. 812.

peace and order to the entire world. The underlying lesson is that learning must begin with the individual. Thus, in understanding what it means to grow up Confucian, the main feature is the emphasis on the role of learning for every person.

The Great Learning has suggested across the centuries that one should look to oneself to correct problems rather than blaming some external cause or some other person. This line of reasoning has both strengths and weaknesses. On the one hand, it demonstrates how important it is for the individual to take responsibility for him- or herself. On the other hand, it may lead someone to blame him- or herself unfairly, failing to recognize an outside cause of a particular problem. This teaching began with Confucius himself, however, who suggested that it was characteristic of the noble person to find fault with himself, whereas it was a trait of the petty person to always blame others. Growing up Confucian meant that one became acculturated to the idea of assuming personal responsibility for one's mistakes and ultimately seeing a broad moral responsibility and obligation to all other people.

FIVE RELATIONS, THREE OBEDIENCES, AND FOUR VIRTUES

For a child growing up in a Confucian home, the process of learning to be a moral person began by acquiring an understanding of the moral basis of various relationships not just within the family, but across all of society. Some of these relationships would be more relevant than others for certain people, but all would provide a foundation for comprehending what constitutes a moral relationship and what behaviors can help someone become moral.

Probably the most-used system of representing these ideal relations was through several groupings of relationships, the most common being the Five Relationships, or *wu-lun*; and the Three Obediences and Four Virtues, or *san-ts'ung ssu-te*. Both of these groupings have long-standing roots in Confucian thought. They are first found in several of the ancient ritual Classics, and they have played a central role throughout the history of Confucianism. The Five Relations focus primarily on men's conduct, while the Three Obediences and Four Virtues are designed specifically for women.

The Five Relations cut across all of society, picking out what are considered to be the most crucial relations that exist, from the ruler down to the common person. These include relationships between ruler and minister, parent and child, husband and wife, older and younger brother, and friend and friend. In each case except the last, the connection is hierarchical, which means it is an unequal association. In such relations, there are moral responsibilities upon each party. For example, as it is the duty of the minister to serve the ruler, it is also the duty of the ruler to care for the minister. With the other sets of social connections, too, there are reciprocal duties placed on each person. While it is the duty of the child to serve the parent, it is the responsibility of the parent to care for the child. Whereas the wife is expected to serve the husband, it is the husband's duty to provide for the wife. Friends are different, in that their bond is on a more equal footing, but even there each person is linked to the other by moral responsibilities. The Five Relations are probably the most essential statement of moral relations in Confucianism. They formed the basis for a broad-based education that was at the center of Confucian teachings.

The Three Obediences and Four Virtues refer more specifically to women and to the particular relationships that have traditionally been considered the center of their lives. The Three Obediences and Four Virtues were the most important set of moral relations for women, and they served as the foundation for women's education in general. The Three Obediences refer specifically to the three relationships that were seen to dominate a women's life in traditional society: First is her relation to her father while she is young and living at home before marriage; second is her connection to her husband after she is married; third is her relationship with her son after her husband has died.

The reason these relations are called the Three Obediences is that, in each case, the woman is viewed as being dependent upon the male—first her father, then her husband, and finally, her son. As in the Five Relations, each relationship involves duties and obligations on the part of the woman to serve the man, but also requires that the man involved provide care for the woman.

The Four Virtues refer to what were once seen as specifically female virtues. They include moral conduct, proper speech, modest appearance, and diligent work. This set of virtues represents traditional society and the conventional roles of women within that society. Such virtues obviously represented a largely subservient role for women and defined their sphere of action as largely limited to domestic life. This subservient role, however, is simply part of the traditional culture in which Confucianism originally operated. Given these gender roles, it is significant that major attention was paid to the continuous process of learning and the role of morality for everyone. From the Confucian perspective, someone who is growing up within the Confucian tradition—whether a boy or a girl—needs to learn to become a moral person.

MORALITY AND NATURAL FEELINGS

For a Confucian child, the principal activity always revolved around learning to become a moral person within the setting of family and society, and in regard to a set of predefined relations held up as the ideal ways in which one might relate to others. What can easily be lost in introducing these steps of learning and ideal moral relations is the degree to which, for Confucians, such feelings were not simply some external code of behavior. Rather, these statements of moral relations represented the basic feelings of human nature. That is, Confucianism taught that morality was not something imposed by an outside source or set up as a code of behavior. Morality was part of human nature itself. These specific forms of behavior and moral relations are seen, then, as natural expressions of the goodness that inherently lies within all men and women.

FILIAL PIETY AND CHILDREN

Moral virtues and relations are nowhere better represented as natural expressions of the goodness of human nature than in the case of filial piety. Though often represented by outsiders as a slavish condition of obedience of the child to the parent, from the Confucian point of view, filial piety reflects the natural love between child and parent. This is not to say that there have not been occasions in history where the relationship has been less than ideal. At its foundations, however, it was intended to express something that, in the Confucian mindset, is a critical indication of the fundamental goodness that Confucians believe constitutes human nature.

If learning is to be found in certain basic and critical moral relations, then, for a child, some of those moral relations are closer and more relevant than others. In either the Five Relations or the Three Obediences, the critical relation for the child is to his or her parents. It is no accident that so much of the instruction intended for children deals with the proper relation with their parents. The discussion of the relationship between children and parents has been a major part of Confucian thought from its inception, and it continues today, as a very broad-based value within the contemporary cultures of East and Southeast Asia. In fact, it might be said that even in those cultures where Confucianism as a recognized tradition plays little continuing role, the conventional Confucian relation of parent and child continues to be seen as a foundational moral value of society.

The moral value in question is what is called filial piety, or *hsiao*. Its discussion in Confucianism begins with Confucius himself. Although the impression often conveyed is that filial piety is a one-way code of behavior that goes from child to parents, with the child having to serve the parents in their every need, Confucius's discussion of the virtue actually suggests a reciprocal relation. Confucius says that filial piety begins with the relation of the parents to the child. In fact, from Confucius's perspective, it is the nurturing and care provided by the parents for the offspring during the child's first several years of life that provide the foundation for the child's future relation to the parents. Because the parents have given the child this care, the child has moral responsibilities to care for his parents in return, especially as they age.

Through the centuries, filial piety has remained one of the central teachings of Confucianism, and the education of children has always emphasized the importance of this virtue. Just about all Confucians of every age have had something to say about filial piety. Early on in the tradition, a short work emerged, called the *Hsiao-ching*, or "Classic of Filial Piety." It not only taught the importance of filial piety, but also suggested that it was the most vital of all virtues and should be considered to be at the very core of all Confucian thought. It also set up a number of basic behaviors now commonly associated with filial piety, particularly the level of obedience that children should show their parents. It was in this work, for example, that the suggestion was made that as long a child's parents are alive, the child should do nothing to put himself in harm's way, nothing to risk any danger, because the body is a gift from the parents, and to bring harm to the body would be to show the parents a lack of respect. In addition, the Classic of Filial Piety suggested that as long as the parents were alive, a child should not travel any great distance so that he would never be far from the parents and thereby would be available to provide for their every need. Although such examples have often been used to criticize Confucian teachings in contemporary Asia, the fact remains that a number of such ideals remain firmly rooted in Confucian cultures even in contemporary times.

FILIAL PIETY—A MODERN EXAMPLE

The centrality of filial piety to Asian culture, and, thus, the degree to which Asian culture reflects Confucian values, is often thought to represent ancient times more than modern ways. The degree to which the concept of filial piety is still a part of contemporary Asian culture can be surprising, however.

An example will illustrate this point. In the early part of my career, my wife and I were living in Japan. We were in a restaurant one evening for dinner and began talking with some of the other customers. They inquired about where we had come from, the length of our stay, and the reason we were living in Japan. We explained that we were in Japan for a year and that our visit had come about because of my career as a scholar of East Asian religions. An individual sitting next to me then asked whether my parents were still alive, a question that initially took me greatly by surprise. My immediate thought was to ask what relevance that had to our stay in Japan. I answered, however, by saying yes, that they were alive. The man then asked if they were with us in Japan. I said no, that my parents were back home, living in the United States. The man's expression was one of great shock. He said that he could not understand how I could be living in Japan while my parents were so far away. I tried to explain that I was married and that my wife and I were now, from our cultural perspective, independent, in a sense, of any immediate obligations to my parents. He asked whether I was not concerned about their well-being and whether I did not feel that I was failing to fulfill my obligation to them by living at such a distance. I began to realize that what I was hearing was a concern that had its roots in very traditional elements of Confucian belief about the importance of filial piety.

The foundation for the point of view that this gentleman expressed was the main teaching found in the Classic of Filial Piety. As long as one's parents are alive, he should not travel far, so that the parents' every need may be attended to. The man in the restaurant was also expressing his concern to me, and not to my wife. The obligation was of the son to his parents, not the daughter to her parents. This particular incident, which I have since seen repeated in many different ways, points to the centrality of filial piety in Asian cultural values and the degree to which Confucianism remains at the heart of that value system. Although in this particular example, the question of filial piety revolved around whether my parents were still alive, the broader concern of the concept reflects the larger belief that duty and responsibility to the parents does not stop with their death; it goes on as the deceased parents continue their role as ancestors. Growing up Confucian means to a large degree becoming knowledgeable about the duties one has toward one's relatives, whether they are living or dead, and the centrality of fulfilling obligations to the family line.

THE ANCESTRAL SHRINE

The most graphic representation of the connection of all family members, both living and dead, is the ancestral shrine, usually referred to as the *tsu miao* ("ancestral shrine") or *chiao miao* ("family shrine"). It is the outward expression of the mutual filial piety and moral obligations that exist between family members. The ancestral shrine was typically a room in one's house or a small separate building. It comprised an altar upon which were placed what are usually known as ancestor tablets, or *shen chu*. These are tablets that bore the name of a deceased family member. The tablets are regarded by many as repositories for the spirit of the departed, particularly at the more popular level of belief and practice. Although Confucians themselves have always taken an agnostic position as to the actual existence of spirits, they do recognize the importance of the tablet as a good mechanism to promote ritual conduct on behalf of the family.

To the child growing up in a Confucian family, the ancestral temple was a symbol of everything that binds the family together as well as a source of comfort and security, and perhaps even awe and some intimidation. Technically speaking, children were not permitted to offer sacrifices to the ancestors until they reached adulthood. With adulthood came the privilege and the responsibility of offering sacrifices and representing family affairs to the departed. It was expected that all major family events would be announced to the departed and that, at times, the ancestors' advice might be sought as well.

A major part of growing up Confucian was coming to understand the importance of the family, the composition of the family, and the responsibility borne by the adult family members

Although for most of his life Confucius was a teacher, for a time he served as a public official in his state's government. He resigned his post after an incident that he felt compromised his moral values, and spent the rest of his days preaching rather than working as a bureaucrat. In the centuries since his death, Confucius has been revered by those who subscribe to his teachings, and he has often been depicted in various forms of art. This bronze statuette shows Confucius in the attire of a mandarin, or public official, relating him to the ancient sage rulers.

Confucius—the scholar, the public official, the founder of the great tradition—has been represented in many different ways in the centuries since he first came to prominence. Perhaps one of the most common—and most accurate—are those depictions that, like this one, show Confucius as a stately man who holds his head high, but as someone who seems more interested in his role as teacher and scholar (note the scrolls he is carrying) than in any recognition by title or position.

Mencius, seen in this ink drawing done in the eighteenth century, became the foremost interpreter of original Confucian thought. He was a disciple of a grandson of Confucius. Although his ideas were not the most influential during his lifetime, after his death, his work, known as the Book of Mencius, later won a place of honor as one of the Four Books.

Filial piety, the concept of a child's devotion and obedience to his parents, is one of the most common themes in Confucianism, and one that is frequently depicted in art. This relief sculpture, believed to have been created sometime between 1127 and 1279, is known as *The Loving Son*. It shows a grown son carrying his elderly parents, taking care of them as they age. The sculpture is one of thousands found on the walls of a series of caves in Ta Tsu, China, that are considered representative of the most impressive achievements in rock carving of the time.

An artist named Yoshitoshi created this ink drawing of Tzu Lu, a disciple of Confucius, in 1888. Tzu Lu was one of the so-called "Twenty-four paragons of filial piety"—a group of Confucians who expressed their views on filial piety in classical ways. Tzu Lu is known as the paragon who carries sacks of rice on his back in order to feed his parents, as he is seen doing here. In this drawing, as Tzu Lu walks along, he studies the teachings of Confucius by the light of the moon. Although he was known to be somewhat brash, Tzu Lu was also a devoted scholar and a brave soldier. He died in battle in 480 B.C. while attempting to put down a rebellion.

Confucian temples, like this beautiful example in Taipei, Taiwan, are marvels of ancient architecture. With their sloping roofs and their ornately decorated interiors, they preserve the traditional artwork and symbolic meanings that were especially important during Confucius's own time.

Temples devoted to Confucius were built with elaborate detail and taken care of with the same devotion that would be shown to an emperor. Not only was a temple a place for worship, but it was also a showcase for extra-ordinary artwork related to religious and political subjects. Many of the decorations in Confucian temples took the form of symbolic creatures, such as dragons, that were also strongly associated with imperial authority. Also common in a Confucian temple are carvings in stone, such as the sculpture of a guard who stands watch over the temple in China's Shantung Province.

In some places, such as Chunghak-dong, South Korea, Confucianism has been preserved as a way of life with very little change from pre-modern times. Confucianism has fit into local practices and folk traditions providing the basis for the people's lifestyle. This photograph, taken in the early 1990s, shows the blending of local religious traditions with Confucianism. Here we have two villagers conducting ritual before a local religious figure. The characters announce the altar as devoted to the Palace of the Immortal with a portrait of the founder of this local religious cult. Such ritual would then be followed by formal ritual at the Confucian Temple, a separate building, but nonetheless connected to the Confucian institution. Such blending of traditions assimilates Confucian teachings and practice to the local lifestyle of a village.

Despite the fact that Confucius died in 479 B.C., the tradition that he began certainly did not die with him. If anything, in the hundreds of years since his death, Confucianism has grown and adapted as necessary to the changing world. Even today, many elements of Confucianism remain an essential part of life in the Asian world. These women, for example, photographed during a Grand Ceremony in 1987, display historical elements of the Confucian tradition through music, dance, and costume. This particular ritual took place at Chongmyo, South Korea, at the Royal Ancestral Shrine.

to maintain family unity through the exercise of proper ritual for departed relatives. At its simplest level, this is a continuation of the most fundamental teaching of Confucianism for children, learning to be a moral person through understanding and practicing filial piety. Ultimately, Confucian teachings themselves always return to the relation of the child to his or her parents. Even when those parents are dead and the child is an old man or woman, the respect and love between them remains, for it is the basis of the Confucian teachings they all share. Learning the foundation of these human relations through an education focused on respect and love is what it means to grow up Confucian.

7

Cultural Expressions and Popular Culture

Follow the calendar of the Hsia dynasty;
ride in the coach of the Shang dynasty;
wear the Chou ceremonial cap;
for music take as model the Shao dance....
                                        —Analects 15:10

As Confucianism grew from its beginnings among a small group of followers of Confucius to the official ideology of the state, and in turn, spread from China into Southeast Asia, Korea, and Japan, it came to represent a broad set of values that applied to virtually every activity within society. This is not to say that there was no role for other teachings and values. Buddhism, Taoism, and Shinto all contributed to the values of certain Asian societies. Confucianism, however, played a role that was far more central to each of these cultures than any other religious tradition.

In societies in which Confucianism played a part, there was virtually no aspect of society unaffected by Confucian teachings and values. Elements of cultural expression and popular culture found in the societies of East and Southeast Asia bear the unmistakable mark of Confucian influence, although there may be a degree of Buddhist, Taoist, or Shinto influence as well. Even in these cases, the Confucian impact very often remains dominant because of its historical central role.

Confucian thought sees cultural forms and popular culture as natural expressions of Confucian values. Whether one is describing painting, poetry, music, or the art of writing, called calligraphy, all cultural expressions may be thought to express Confucian values in profound ways. In turn, there is an understanding of popular culture as rooted in the high culture of the teachings of the sages and the literature that represents their values. Although there may be a great distance between that high culture and its most common cultural expressions, there is still a tie. From the Confucian point of view, the connection is critical, because popular culture can ideally be viewed as a continuation of higher-level teachings and their values.

For cultural expressions in the arts, the connection to Confucian values rests in the definition of beauty. Whether one is dealing with painting, poetry, music, or calligraphy, each art form possesses something that one might describe as beauty or artistic value. The question, then, is how Confucianism defines or understands beauty.

Not surprisingly, Confucian definitions of beauty incorporate the moral values that lie at the foundation of Confucian teachings. Any definition of beauty embodies *jen* ("humaneness"), *I* ("righteousness"), *li* ("ritual" or "propriety"), and *hsiao* ("filial piety"), perhaps not literally, but in terms of their connections to moral value generally. Beauty is thoroughly moral. At a more subtle level of philosophical meaning, as seen in the development of Neo-Confucianism, beauty becomes a more thorough reflection on the understanding of Confucian teachings. In probing more deeply into human nature and the state of the universe, the Neo-Confucians saw moral structure in all things, what they called *li*, or "principle," the moral nature of Heaven in every aspect of the individual, the world, and the universe. From this point of view, cultural expression and popular culture become expressions or manifestations of this underlying moral nature of the universe, the Way of Heaven. The degree to which artists are successful in this expression depends on the extent to which they represent both what is beautiful and what is good.

CALLIGRAPHY

Calligraphy refers to the art of writing—not so much the content of the writing as the form of writing itself. The way in which one writes is judged to be an artistic expression. Most of us today pay little attention to the appearance of what we write. In fact, many of us "write" only on our computers—even our correspondence is done by e-mail. In premodern societies, however, writing was regarded very highly for its potential artistic expression. In China, the art of writing has a very long history, and it is equally important in Southeast Asia as well as Korea and Japan. In fact, calligraphy traces back at least to the Chou Dynasty in China, where it was regarded as one of the so-called Six Arts, the disciplines thought necessary for the education of every cultured person.

Across the centuries, calligraphy has continued to be held in very high esteem, to the point where it has come to be seen as a major form of artistic expression. Though it might typically be viewed as a product of high culture, it actually has immense popularity across a wide spectrum. There have been many individual masters of the art of calligraphy. Often, their works will be studied at great length in order to understand the techniques they employ and to appreciate the artistic skill they display. The great masters of calligraphy have always been singled out for particular recognition and praise. In contemporary times, it is not uncommon to see an exhibition of calligraphy by major museums, both in Asia and abroad.

At the more popular level, individuals from all parts of society practice calligraphy, hoping to achieve a degree of artistic expression that they or perhaps their friends or teacher will believe rises to the level of the beauty of the art. It is not uncommon in Asia to see old men in parks in the early morning practicing calligraphy with a large brush, using only water on the cement of the sidewalks. Passersby will stand, silent and reverential, and watch as the art is created before their eyes. It is exciting to watch as the writing covers cement block after cement block, and then, as quickly as it has been created, disappears under the rays of the warming sun.

What does one write when engaging in calligraphy? Is one writing expressions that are made up as one goes along? Or is it simply a random sequence of Chinese characters? The answer is neither. Most frequently, calligraphers copy some famous literary passage. Historically, the source of such quotations has been classical literature, although many other sources are possible, such as a famous poem. Calligraphy is not necessarily a Confucian art per se. After all, anyone with any point of view can practice the art of writing. A Buddhist would most likely write phrases from one of the Buddhist scriptures, and a Taoist from Taoist scriptures.

What is the connection of this art form to Confucian values? A master of calligraphy will be described as someone who understands the way of the brush, who is able to express the connection of the written form of the individual character to the broader set of moral values of the Confucian tradition.

Certainly, part of the meaning of engaging in calligraphy for the practitioner is the value believed to be found in the copying of phrases from a source that is judged to be of moral worth. At the level of a master, however, calligraphy reflects on the nature of the practitioner. It is said that it can express the inner moral nature—and so, a true master of the art will be seen as embodying a sense of moral goodness. To evaluate these qualities is a form of artistic judgment about what constitutes beauty. In the Confucian case, the master's calligraphy is both beautiful and good because the judgment of what makes something beautiful is the fact that its moral goodness is visible.

LITERATURE

Literature is a very broad category in any culture. China, Korea, and Japan are no exception to this rule. There have been many forms of literature throughout the history of these cultures, and a number of those can be discussed in relation to Confucian teachings and values. Probably the two most prominent types are poetry and fictional literature. Each bears the mark of Confucian influence, though they may have different motives and different results.

Poetry

The model for the understanding of all poetry from a Confucian perspective was the *Shih ching*, the Classic or Book of Poetry. This collection of more than three hundred poems stood as the foundation for the understanding of poetry and, from the Confucian point of view, represented perfection in the poetic art. The fact that it became one of the Five Classics suggests the importance that subsequent generations of Confucians placed on the work. One can still ask, however, what it was that Confucians saw as the value of this collection of poems.

There can be no doubt that the Book of Poetry is an extraordinary collection of poems representing virtually all aspects of life in the early Chou Dynasty. There are courtly ballads, dynastic accounts, and founding legends and myths. In addition, because a number of the poems seem to have had their origins in folk songs and ballad traditions, some are about topics that include features of popular life, romantic relationships, and even forms of social protest against cruel and tyrannical rule. Is it this wide range of topics and the invaluable insight into the life of the early Chou Dynasty that led the Confucians to value the collection so highly? The answer is no.

For the Confucians, the poems were important because they could be viewed as an embodiment of Confucian moral teachings. Speaking of the Book of Poetry, Confucius stated that all of the three hundred poems might be summarized with a single phrase: There are no evil thoughts to be found anywhere in the work. One of Confucius's disciples went into more detail, describing the poetry as responsible for establishing standards of right and wrong and as capable of guiding humans in proper relationships and providing general moral education to all segments of society.

Every poem, at least in the eyes of the Confucians, has a moral lesson—even those poems that, on the surface, are clearly steeped in romantic love and courtship. For the Confucian, such poems are not really about romantic love. Rather, they serve as allegories for proper relations between, for example, the subject and the ruler or the minister and the ruler. Each poem demonstrates the purity of morality that was believed to have existed in early Chou times. For the Confucian, such morality is the great lesson of the work and what makes it so important for later generations.

With the Book of Poetry as a model, the Confucian tradition sought the same standards in all verse. Confucianism focused first and foremost on the moral nature of the poem and the degree to which it could help advance the reader's moral education. Poetry should not be written simply for the pure pleasure of the art. It had to teach a moral lesson; otherwise, it had no artistic value. Poetry that was licentious and lewd or frivolous and lighthearted was simply cast aside as unworthy of study at all. For the Confucian, a good poem was a moral poem.

Fictional Literature

Most of what we have discussed thus far as either Confucian literature or Confucian-influenced literature represents high culture that was prevalent among the educated few. The Five Classics and the Four Books primarily describe a literature that was the product of the upper classes and was largely aimed at the education of the elite. The same may be said of poetry in general, and certainly of its study and composition. The case is very different when one looks at fictional literature, which includes not only novels, but also drama and the rich traditions of oral fiction in storytellers and even puppet theater. Such literature was very much the voice of the common people, and it would often take a position that mocked the ways of those who espoused the high culture. Often, pieces of popular fictional literature were written anonymously, for fear of reprisals should the author of a work be identified by the authorities.

Did Confucian teachings and values permeate the world of popular literature as well as the high culture, or was Confucianism more limited in its appeal to the common people? In other words, if fictional literature often made fun of high culture, was Confucianism made fun of, too? How, in turn, did Confucians view this popular art form? Did fictional literature, like the works of high culture, serve as a role model for moral education?

To the Confucian, even fictional literature had to be of moral value. There was simply no time for real leisure or entertainment for its own sake. It was imperative that everything include a moral lesson. In the world of popular culture and literature, the heroes of stories sometimes abided by the moral path, but in other cases they did not. These were, after all, works that focused on the common people and their lives, and the stories portrayed people in all their desires and passions.

They could be violent, antisocial, antiestablishment, sensuous, and even pornographic—and they were often great tales that were widely read and enjoyed. Tales with "immoral" protagonists or themes, however, fell outside the acceptable realm of moral conduct from the Confucian perspective, and were regarded as unworthy of study. At times, Confucians even made efforts to ban them as seditious. Some popular literature did poke fun at the Confucians themselves, which was certainly not appreciated by those for whom moral education was the central agenda.

Even though it incorporated some unconventional themes, popular literature very often sought to ground itself in general Confucian teachings. Such Confucian values were often mixed with Buddhist and Taoist ideas as well, but Confucianism emerged as a foundation for many of the moral lessons found in major fictional writing. There is, for example, the Confucian hero. This is an individual who selflessly seeks the cause of the right, often against terrible odds. Evil—often depicted in the form of a tyrannical emperor, a hated and corrupt minister of state, or a foreign invader—was seen as the enemy that lies in the path of the humble and righteous Confucian whose only intention is to do good for others. The portrayal of Confucian values was not always so dramatic, though. Often, tales focused on the loyal Confucian minister, the filial son, the faithful wife, the support of the family and the ancestors, or loyalty to the emperor. All of these relationships depicted Confucian teachings and values, and, to a large degree, they formed the bedrock for the literature that best depicted popular life in Asian societies.

ART

Art, like literature, is a very broad category. Given the limitations of space, it is best to focus on a single art form in order to fully understand the relation between art and Confucian teachings. Probably the most famous art form—and one that has received extensive commentary—is painting.

Painting raises a number of important questions, not the least of which is the nature of the Confucian influence. It also brings up the question of the nature of the influence of any religious tradition on this type of artistic work. It allows us to look also at the relation between a visual form and a form of teaching. Simply put, how does a visual form express a particular teaching or set of values? Short of depicting religious subject matter itself, such as a Buddhist monk, a Taoist hermit, or a Confucian scholar, what is it about a painting—of a landscape, for example—that would identify it as Buddhist, Taoist, or Confucian?

When Chinese painting, particularly landscape painting, is discussed, there is often a tendency to see Buddhist or Taoist influences. In the case of Korean or Japanese painting, there would be a strong sense of Buddhist influence. What is frequently not mentioned, however, is the influence of Confucianism. If we think of a standard East Asian landscape painting, we see mountains, mist, perhaps a waterfall, a river, a lake, or a small pavilion with a diminutive person. Such views are said to represent the infinity of time and space, the vastness of nature, and the smallness of humankind. Such qualities are considered Buddhist or Taoist—certainly not Confucian. Yet these paintings, called *wen-jen hua*, or literati painting, are very often the products of Confucians! Assuming that the work is not done by a Confucian who has decided to take a moment to look at the world through the eyes of a Buddhist or Taoist, there must be something about such paintings that makes them Confucian. What is it?

The answer, in large part, rests not with the subject portrayed in the painting, but with the mind and heart of the artist. One cannot always paint subject matter that is visibly moral in content. There are only so many family settings displaying filial piety, and there are a limited number of views of a loyal minister. But how does one bring a Confucian focus to a landscape, which, unlike a person, has no apparent moral nature? The moral nature involved is primarily that of the painter, which is reflected in the painting. The work of art is a reflection of this moral character. The subject matter, then, is limitless. A landscape can reflect the painter's Confucian vision of the world, of the infinite moral order of *li* in all things under *T'ien*.

What about painting and popular culture? Again, we have been describing painting principally as it relates to high culture. More popular and folk traditions of painting tended to focus on the subject matter itself. A painting that is influenced by Confucianism has Confucian themes as part of its subject. For example, in East Asian folk art there is a tradition of using a Chinese character within the painting. A painting might be composed of the character *hsiao*, representing filial piety. This is not calligraphy because the character is only one part of the painting. Painted within and around the character would be perhaps five or six small scenes, each depicting some example of filial piety. One might be a filial son serving an aging parent. Another might be a young parent taking care of a child. Still another might be people caring for animals, harvesting a crop, or making a sacrificial offering to ancestors. In each case, the meaning of filial piety—or some other Confucian value—is expressed through examples from everyday life.

MUSIC

Music, too, has played a very important role in the Confucian tradition, a role reinforced by references to the lost sixth Confucian Classic that was supposedly devoted to the subject of music. Music was regarded as one of the Six Arts, the foundation for the education of any cultured person. An important piece of early writing, *Yüeh chi*, or Records of Music, is now a chapter in the *Li Chi*, or Book of Rites, which is one of the Five Classics. The Records of Music expounds the meaning and importance of music.

From the Confucian perspective, music was a product of the sage rulers of antiquity, just like various codes of moral behavior. According to the Confucians, everything transmitted from the sage rulers to the present generation was part of the Way of *T'ien*, and thus, part of the moral rule the sages established.

Therefore, the sages' rituals were part of the moral order—and so was their music. Music and ritual were both believed to display a form of order and structure that reflected the order of everything under Heaven. Music could not exist without its internal structure of melody and harmony. It contains an ordered structure of notes, and by playing it or even hearing it, Confucians believed that one entered into the order and harmony that music represented. Confucius made it abundantly clear that music reflects moral values when he said in the Confucian Analects that a person who is not morally good would have no association with music. For this reason, music was seen as a way to engage in moral learning, and Confucius encouraged musical education because of what he saw as music's redeeming moral qualities. Music was, to Confucius, a form of moral learning.

Because of the long relation of the Confucians with the classical literature and ceremony, the understanding of music has been permeated historically with Confucian influence. However, this encouragement and praise of music also had limitations for the Confucians. Confucius was very adamant about the moral character of the music of the ancients. He was equally adamant about the music of his own day. He found many musical forms morally reprehensible and licentious, and argued strenuously for a return to the music of the ancients. In the Confucian Analects, one of the rulers Confucius advises confesses his fondness for the music of his own day and his inability to take an interest in the music of the ancients. Confucius and his followers remain undeterred, insisting that the music of the ancients was a source of moral learning and that contemporary music had few redeeming qualities.

Of course, for more contemporary Confucians, the issue is far more complex, but the relation of even a contemporary Confucian to more popular forms of music is problematic, simply because of the overarching Confucian need to see music as fulfilling its moral capacity. In theory, only where lyrics would complement Confucian teachings or where the music itself represented the traditional ideals of harmony and order would there be a Confucian endorsement of contemporary musical expression. This suggests, of course, that much modern music might stand at odds with Confucian teachings and values, though even today the potential for permeation of such values continues to be present, just as it was through the centuries of Confucian history.

8

Social Reinforcement of Confucian Values

It is always true that rites,
when they serve the living, are an adornment to joy,
and when they serve the dead, an adornment to grief.
In sacrifices they are an adornment to reverence,
and in military affairs, an adornment to authority.
This was the same for the rites of the hundred kings;
it is what unites antiquity and the present.

—Hsün Tzu, "Li-lun"

A number of institutions in East and Southeast Asia were responsible for the social reinforcement of Confucian values. The Confucian Temple, for example, with its history of the Twice Yearly Ceremony, acted as a means of displaying Confucian teachings, values, and ritual in a public fashion. The family, too, has been an important means of implementation and reinforcement of Confucian values. The ancestral shrine was, in many respects, the very center of such familial reinforcement. Though the family ritual within the ancestral shrine was a very private expression of the Confucian tradition, it still acted as one of the most influential, if not *the* most influential, way to reinforce Confucianism. It was, after all, in the family that the teaching of Confucian values began. It was also in the setting of the special relations represented by the family that the most important form of moral obligations and responsibility was demonstrated.

In addition to the Confucian Temple and the family and its ancestral shrine, there are other ways Confucian teachings and values are reinforced in society. These may be found in holidays; in various rites of passage, such as capping, a ritual that represents a boy's achievement of manhood; in weddings, childbirths, and funerals; in the educational system; in the civil service examination system; and simply in the social ethics of acting and living within society.

HOLIDAYS

When one thinks of a particular religion, often the best-known feature of the tradition is the holidays that its participants celebrate. Holidays may be the most commonly known element of a religion for both participants and nonparticipants alike because, in many respects, they are the most public display of the tradition and its heritage. For example, Christmas and Easter are often the best-known aspects of Christianity. In Judaism, it would be Passover and Rosh Hashanah. In Islam, it would be the holy month of Ramadan. These holidays or holy periods represent something very significant within each religious tradition. They commemorate a special event or moment in time. As such, they are viewed as holy—religious holidays, or "holy days."

In Confucianism, once again, there is a very different sense of what constitutes its religious nature. As a result, it is far more difficult to pinpoint particular events or moments in time that have the same sense of the religious or holy about them as do the holidays of other religious traditions. This is also not to say that there are no holidays in cultures that have practiced Confucianism. For example, historically, the Lunar New Year festival is a major holiday period in Asia; so, too, is the Mid-Autumn Festival, as well as a variety of other events and holidays. Because of the dominance of Confucian values as official state orthodoxy in these cultures, most common holidays have certain Confucian values attached to them. Does this, however, make them Confucian holidays? Not really. There is nothing in these holidays that is celebrated as a specific and essential feature of the Confucian tradition itself.

There is one holiday that *can* be clearly described as Confucian, but it, too, has a unique twist that once again differentiates it from the holidays of other religious traditions. That holiday is Confucius's Birthday. It is celebrated on September 28 and corresponds with Teacher's Day, the day on which all teachers are venerated for the value of their contributions to education and learning.

The unusual character of this holiday comes from the fact that Confucius is recognized on a day devoted to the celebration of education and learning in general. In other words, this holiday is not first and foremost a celebration of Confucius and his birth, but rather of teachers in general, with the recognition that Confucius was a teacher. It is important to see the difference between this holiday and the holidays of other religious traditions. Although Confucius receives wide acclaim, he is not singled out and venerated in a fashion that would highlight the holiness of the founder of a religion. He is simply being recognized as a teacher—the first teacher—with nothing miraculous or supernatural being implied in regard to his birth.

This recognition of Confucius is the only true Confucian holiday. Though it differs greatly from other religious holidays, it does serve to reinforce the role and importance given to learning and education in general. More important still, it firmly connects education with Confucius, thus ensuring the link between learning and Confucian teachings and values.

LIFE PASSAGE RITUALS

Every human being passes through certain basic stages of life from birth to death. Transitions from one stage of life to the next form the basis for fundamental rituals. Within the context of Confucianism, rituals became methods of social reinforcement of Confucian values. These included rituals of birth, marriage, capping, and funerals.

Rituals associated with birth reinforced the importance of continuing the family line, and the confirmation of sacrifice to the ancestors. Rituals associated with marriage also emphasized the importance of the family line and the creation of new life within the family, as well as the obligations between husband and wife.

The ritual of capping, a coming-of-age ceremony, represented a boy's transition to manhood. It is performed by a ceremonial changing of childhood clothes for adult clothes. Adult clothing includes a cap worn on the head (for males). During this ritual, the child is initiated to this headdress. This event generally corresponded to the end of the teenage years, although for a member of the imperial family, it usually took place at the beginning of the teen years. The custom goes back to early ritual texts; because it is part of the Classics, it became a central ceremony in the Confucian tradition. Both Hsün Tzu and Chu Hsi commented on its value. The ritual is significant because it represents the completion of childhood, an event symbolized by the wearing of adult clothes and the first formal presentation to the ancestors in the ancestral hall.

Confucian values were also reinforced through funerals. For a Confucian, the funeral was a critically important ritual at which people displayed their feelings for the lost relative. Every last element of the ceremony was detailed, as were the differences that marked the ceremonies, depending upon the class and status of the family involved. Confucians spent great time and effort commenting in ritual manuals on all the details associated with funerals. Such details include how and for how long to observe mourning, what clothes should be worn, which family members may be involved and to what degree, the preparation of the body for burial, the preparation of the ancestral tablet for placement in the ancestral temple, and the selection of the burial spot. For example, the classic Confucian understanding of how to mourn the loss of one's parents meant that the surviving child would mourn by the gravesite for over two years. It is remarkable that prominent Confucians through history actually found the time to carry out this ritual of mourning. The Confucian values associated with this ritual process chiefly focus upon the filial piety shown toward the departed and the Confucian importance placed upon ritual itself as the moral order of society.

EDUCATION OF CHILDREN

In East and Southeast Asian culture, education plays a central role in the life of each individual; it is considered without doubt the most-sought value. One fundamental teaching of Confucianism is the belief that learning should be available to all people and that everyone has the capability of pursuing learning with hard work and diligence. To say that, traditionally, all education was Confucian education meant that each part of the learning process from the elementary level right through the university was dominated by Confucian teachings as found in the Classics and in Confucian interpretations of a wide range of literary sources, from novels to poetry and even to the writings of other religious traditions, such as Taoism and Buddhism.

From the Sung Dynasty to the twentieth century, children's education began with several works that introduced basic Confucian values. The first of these works, called the *Ch'ien tzu wen*, or "Thousand Character Essay," was composed by an official during the Liang Dynasty in the early sixth century. It became a standard educational work during the Sung Dynasty. It comprised a thousand characters (symbols that form words in Chinese), as the title suggests, and taught basic knowledge about a variety of subjects. Although some later Confucians believed it was not "Confucian enough" in its content, it did stress the value of education and the importance of moral lessons, and it contributed in significant ways to the foundation of Confucian learning.

The second work that formed the basis of Confucian learning was the *San Tzu Ching*, or "Three Character Classic." Composed during the thirteenth century, it became a staple work in the Confucian curriculum. Written in a style that was very easy to memorize—three-character lines—it taught basic Confucian values, stressing the moral character of learning and Mencius's belief in the goodness of human nature, and placing a particular focus on the importance of the virtue of filial piety.

MEN'S LEARNING—SCHOOLS AND DEGREES

For the male, social reinforcement of Confucian values came about in large part through the increasing levels of higher education and the pursuit of advanced degrees and examinations. It meant studying a standard curriculum of the works of Confucian scripture: the Five Classics in the periods prior to the advent of Neo-Confucianism, and both the Five Classics and the Four Books after the development of Neo-Confucianism.

Though there are many differences in the system of learning used from one historical period to another, in broad outline education began at the local level, with the student advancing from primary school to regional and provincial schools, and finally to the national university. Some individuals opted to study in private schools and academies. Higher education was the pathway to personal advancement and success: More positions became available in the government bureaucracy with each succeeding level of education. Whichever educational route was chosen, success was measured by performance on the examinations that were given to students to assess their level of education.

A series of examinations was established as early as the seventh century. These were generally known as the civil service examination system, and they continued to be used up to the twentieth century. At both the local and national level, these examinations became the basis for the measure of success. Education at the local level was tested through what was called either a Prefectural Examination or a Provincial Examination. The national level had two examinations: the Metropolitan Examination and the Palace Examination, the latter of which represented the highest level. The Palace Examination represented the highest and most prestigious examination, the *chin shih*, or Presented Scholar Examination. If a man achieved a superior score, he was assured of a high-level position in the government and might potentially advance to play a key role in political administration. The degree of education achieved also determined which individuals played major roles in the educational system.

At the heart of it, the Confucian educational system did not differ dramatically from our own system of higher education. What makes the system different was the content of the learning. The foundation of the entire system rested upon a curriculum that was Confucian in content. Confucian teachings permeated all aspects of education within society. Even the knowledge required to pass the civil service examination was Confucian in content. Whereas we generally view civil service examinations for government jobs as primarily a way to test technical skills, the Confucian perspective was very different. Throughout Confucian history, civil service examinations scarcely ever involved technical skills. Rather, they were examinations that tested what we might consider the humanities. They assessed someone's understanding of Confucian interpretations of literature and philosophy. The examinations, culminating in the *chin shih*, required a thorough knowledge of the Confucian Classics, as well as advanced skills such as the ability to compose prose and poetry. Was this any way to put together a civil service examination to test for government jobs? The system was, in fact, used over a period of some 1,400 years, and although no one would argue that it didn't have certain problems, it actually produced a very large number of highly qualified civil servants, ministers of state, and educational administrators.

WOMEN'S LEARNING—DOMESTIC MORALITY

Although women were excluded from the formal path to success offered to men by way of the civil service examination system, the education available to them was regarded as a very important aspect of Confucianism. Despite the fact that, for much of the history of Confucianism, the tradition generally saw fit to subject women to a position inferior to that of men, this did not minimize the importance attributed to learning for women.

Because Confucians believed that learning was important for all people, a tradition of education for women was established by the Han Dynasty. An important writing by the prominent female Confucian Pan Chao during the Han period, the *Nü Chieh*, or "Commandments for Women," was addressed to Pan Chao's daughters. It sought to introduce the moral responsibilities of women, arguing the importance of the Three Obediences and Four Virtues as the foundation for how women should live. Even though women were considered inferior to men, Confucianism suggested a balance of *yin* and *yang*, or male and female, which emphasized that each sex was equally important to the harmony of the world.

On the basis of Pan Chao's work, others appeared: the *Nü hsiao ching*, or "Book of Filial Piety for Women"; *Nü lun yü*, or "Analects for Women"; *Nei hsün*, or "Instructions for the Inner Quarters"; and *Nü-fan chieh lu*, or "A Concise Account of Basic Regulations for Women." Eventually, four of these works were combined into the *Nü-ssu-shu*, or "Four Books for Women," which was created as a counterpart to the Four Books, the standard for the education of men. The *Ssu-shu* was organized by the great Sung Neo-Confucian Chu Hsi.

WOMEN'S EDUCATION

A number of works were written that focused specifically on the education of women. They introduced women to basic Confucian teachings and values in a world still dominated by men. Thus, the virtues referred to in the following writing must be viewed as very old-fashioned ways of discussing the role of women, and they certainly suggest subservience to the male. On the other hand, they also reveal the degree to which education was being made available to women and the extent to which women were thought capable of perfecting their moral natures just as men were. This particular passage comes from a work called *Nei hsün*, "Instructions for the Inner Quarters," a work composed by the Empress Hsü, wife of the third Ming Dynasty Emperor Cheng Tzu (who ruled 1402–1424). The aim of the work was to provide women with a guide to learning to cultivate their moral natures.

> Being upright and modest, reserved and quiet, correct and dignified, sincere and honest: these constitute the moral nature of a woman. Being filial and respectful, humane and perspicacious, loving and warm, meek and gentle: these represent the complete development of the moral nature. The moral nature being innate in our endowment, it becomes transformed and fulfilled through practice. It is not something that comes from outside but is actually rooted in our very selves.
>
> Of old, upright women ordered their feelings and nature based upon moral principle (*li*), kept control over the workings of their mind, and honored the Way and its virtue. Therefore they were able to complement their gentlemen [husbands] in fulfilling the teachings of the Way. This is the reason they took humaneness to be their abode, rightness as their path of action, wisdom as their guide, trustworthiness as their defense, and ritual decorum as the embodiment of it. . . .

* William Theodore de Bary and Irene Bloom, comp., *Sources of Chinese Tradition*, 2nd ed., vol. 1, New York: Columbia University Press, 1999, pp. 834–835.

ACTING IN SOCIETY—SOCIAL ETHICS

Ultimately, Confucian teachings and values were reinforced through participation in society itself. We have seen the importance of the Great Learning as a guide to the Confucian educational process. The Great Learning emphasizes the growth of the individual and his internal nature, but the goal of the text and of Confucianism itself remains peace in the world. As the individual becomes a moral person, he or she acts in ways that bring morality to any situation in which they are involved. Simply put, there is no action that should not be a moral action, and if all people would conduct themselves with an eye to moral values, then there would be peace in the world because the world would be a moral one.

9

Defining Moments in Confucian History

If heaven intended to destroy this culture, later mortals
such as I would not have been able to share in it.

—Analects 9:5

onfucianism, as we have seen, has existed for approximately twenty-five hundred years and covers a wide area of cultural territory in both East Asia and Southeast Asia. In spite of that expanse, both chronologically and spatially, it is possible to pick out a handful of defining moments that have taken place in Confucian history. Each of these events set the stage for significant changes within the tradition and contributed to the modern understanding of the nature of the tradition as it exists today.

MENCIUS ON HUMAN NATURE

Though he was little known in his own generation, as the centuries passed Mencius (Meng Tzu) became the principal interpreter of Confucius's teachings. The elevation of Mencius to this revered status occurred during the development of Neo-Confucianism, mainly during the Sung period. Symbolic of this newfound role within the tradition, the works of Mencius were paired with Confucius's writings in the Four Books, the foundation of all major Confucian learning that came later.

Mencius's most basic contribution to the Confucian tradition—and the one that represents a defining moment for the tradition as a whole—is his argument for the goodness of human nature. In a debate with another philosopher of his day, Mencius presented his belief in the goodness of human nature, which became a central tenet of Confucian thought.

Mencius's opponent in the discussion of human nature was the philosopher Kao Tzu. We know nothing about this individual other than what we learn from his discussions with Mencius. There is no separate body of Kao Tzu's writings. His debates with Mencius, however, highlight several opposing views of human nature and help explain the viewpoint that eventually dominated all of Confucian thought.

Kao Tzu began by arguing that human nature may be compared to the wood of the willow tree, while moral virtue or goodness may be seen as a wooden cup or basket that has been made out of the tree's wood. Whereas the cup and basket are items made of wood, the wood itself is raw material. It is only

THE CHILD AND THE WELL

One of the most famous passages from the writings of Mencius involves the story of a child about to fall into a well. Mencius uses this incident to discuss his fundamental belief in the goodness of human nature. He argues that any human being who saw a child about to fall into a well would rescue the child from danger. From its first appearance in the work of Mencius, this tale has been repeated and referenced over hundreds of years of Confucian writings. It is a basic incident that produces for almost everyone a confirmation of Mencius's own interpretation—yes, anyone seeing a child at the edge of a well would try to rescue the child. For Mencius, of course, the story suggests the more profound observation that a human being would rescue the child because of the inherent goodness in his or her nature. Mencius's argument is that this goodness is not the product of external learning, but of human nature itself in its pure form.

All human beings have a mind that cannot bear to see the sufferings of others . . . Here is why I say that all human beings have a mind that commiserates with others. Now, if anyone were suddenly to see a child about to fall into a well, his mind would be filled with alarm, distress, pity, and compassion. That he would react accordingly is not because he would use the opportunity to ingratiate himself with the child's parents, nor because he would seek commendation from neighbors and friends, nor because he would hate the adverse reputation. From this it may be seen that one who lacks a mind that feels pity and compassion would not be human; one who lacks a mind that feels shame and aversion would not be human; one who lacks a mind that feels modesty and compliance would not be human; and one who lacks a mind that knows right and wrong would not be human. The mind's feeling of pity and compassion is the beginning of humaneness . . . the mind's feeling of shame and aversion is the beginning of rightness . . . the mind's feeling of modesty and compliance is the beginning of propriety; and the mind's sense of right and wrong is the beginning of wisdom. Human beings have these four beginnings just as they have four limbs.*

* William Theodore de Bary and Irene Bloom, comp., *Sources of Chinese Tradition*, 2nd ed., vol. 1, New York: Columbia University Press, 1999, p.129.

through the act of working with the original wood that items such as cups and baskets are made. In turn, Kao Tzu argued, moral goodness is not an inherent part of human nature, but something that must be added. It is the product of working with the raw material of human existence. To become a moral person, according to Kao Tzu, requires the same effort as carving cups or making baskets from wood.

In response, Mencius states that Kao Tzu's argument suggests that end products are the result of a substantial change in the raw material itself, and that end products are made at the expense of raw material. He says that this would mean that the creation of cups and baskets is, in a sense, a violation of the wood, since it would have to be substantially transformed to render the final product. To extend this idea to human nature, Mencius asked, must we create moral goodness by violating human nature itself? Mencius argues that moral goodness is basic to human beings, and is not the product of outside forces that are brought to bear upon the raw material of human nature.

Kao Tzu next argued that human nature is like the flow of water. The water will flow in whatever direction a channel is opened—east, west, north, or south. Like water, human nature will flow in whatever direction a channel is opened. This argument suggests that human nature is neither good nor evil, but is entirely dependent upon the external forces acting upon it. If a channel opens in the direction of good, then human nature will become good. If the channel is the opposite, then human nature will become evil.

Mencius responds to this argument by agreeing that water can flow as easily to the east as to the west, but then he asks whether it can flow uphill just as well as it can flow downhill. Of course, the answer is no: Water, without external force acting on it, only flows downhill. It is the same, Mencius argues, with human nature. That is, human nature is morally good, just as it is in the nature of water to flow downward. Mencius goes on to argue that, although water can be forced to run uphill by way of a series of dams, to do this is not in the true nature of the water. It is the same with human nature. People, too, can be forced to act against their own nature—to commit evil—but such action is a violation of their true nature.

These arguments and several more like them became the basis for the fundamental Confucian belief in the goodness of human nature. Mencius's position became the most basic and agreed-upon understanding. Even in contemporary times, his position remains the foundation for Confucian thinking about what makes up human nature. Particularly as Confucianism attempts to define a role for itself in the modern age, this question of human nature and the arguments of Mencius remain central to any consideration of the future of Confucianism.

BURNING BOOKS AND BURYING SCHOLARS

Two events that form a watershed for the Confucian tradition are linked to the cruelty of the first emperor of the short-lived Ch'in Dynasty (221–207 B.C.), Ch'in Shih Huang-ti. Though the events are separated by a year, they are usually discussed together as examples of the extremes to which the emperor would go in his efforts to guarantee his power and prevent any dissension within the empire. Confucians were on the receiving end of both these events, which had profound effects on the future development of the tradition.

The first of these events, the "burning of the books," or *fen shu,* is said to have taken place in 213 B.C. at the command of the emperor. Numerous volumes dealing with a range of subjects were collected and burned. Only books that dealt with medicine, divination, and agriculture, as well as materials related to the history of the Ch'in Dynasty itself, were spared. The only other exception was made for the Confucian literati, who were allowed to retain copies of the Book of Poetry and the Book of History. No one else, however, was allowed to own these volumes. As a matter of retaining a record of the destroyed works, a copy of each volume to be burned was kept in two locations. This procedure should have allowed for the preservation of two copies of every work of the vast corpus of literature that was otherwise burned. The plan, in fact, would have succeeded had both depositories not been destroyed during the fighting that came with the fall of the Ch'in Dynasty. As a result of this destruction, many volumes of literature were lost forever.

What lay behind this massive destruction of literary sources? The emperor was advised by his Prime Minister Li Ssu that if he wanted to gain complete control and suppress all opposition, then it would be best to eliminate all diversity of thought. This would allow the state to wield unprecedented authority, to control all education, and to mold public opinion. The tragedy of the book burning would have been significant enough as an example of the largely successful thought control carried out under the authoritarian rule of the Ch'in Dynasty, even if it had not led to the permanent loss of so many literary works. The Ch'in Dynasty, after all, did not last long, and as tragic as the event might have been to the people who went through it, after the establishment of peace and order under the Han Dynasty, the burning's impact might have been overcome if the two copies of the works set aside had been preserved as originally intended.

The second event, the "burying of the scholars," or *k'ung ju*, is said to have taken place in 212 B.C., also at the command of Emperor Ch'in Shih Huang-ti. According to the major historical record of the period, *Shih chi*, or "Records of the Historian," more than 460 scholars were gathered together and slaughtered at the Ch'in capital of Hsien-yang.

There are, as one might expect, many conflicting stories about this event. Traditionally, the interpretation has stressed that the scholars were buried alive, though modern research has come to shed some doubt on that. Few historians dispute, however, that a very large number of scholars were indeed slaughtered.

One question often posed is whether the scholars killed were strictly Confucians or whether they represented the whole range of thought of the day. The Records of the Historian seems to suggest that those targeted were primarily Confucians. The decision to bury the scholars was supposedly the result of mounting public criticism of the emperor's actions—particularly his cruelty. Again, the act was intended to silence criticism and to guarantee complete imperial authority and uniformity of thought among the people.

These two events were pivotal to the later history of Confucianism in several ways. First, the burning of the books resulted in a great deal of confusion within the Confucian tradition and within the entire Chinese literary tradition. After the demise of the Ch'in Dynasty, texts began to appear that were said to have been hidden during the persecution period. Often, different versions of the same text would appear. (We have referred to these already as New Text and Old Text versions.) They presented vastly differing images of Confucius and the major ideas of the tradition. Although the Old Text versions have generally been accepted as the more accurate, the legacy of the burning of the books has left the Confucian tradition with a complex textual history that, given the emphasis placed on the literary classics, made the task of unraveling the meaning of these sources quite difficult.

Second, the burying of the scholars created a heritage of martyrdom for those Confucians who upheld the tradition of dissent. Confucian ministers of state served the emperor directly, and also worked in virtually every other level of government. These officials believed that they were playing a critical role in advising the emperor on the proper course of action, on the basis of understanding the moral ways of the ancient rulers. In practical terms, this role meant that the Confucian often acted as the conscience or moral arbiter for the ruler. The burying of the scholars was a stark reminder of the risks of providing this kind of moral advice.

Both the burning of the books and the burying of the scholars set the tone for the future role Confucians envisioned for themselves. Confucianism would continue to stress learning and moral responsibility as the way to combat the greed and cruelty associated with an authoritarian regime like that of the Ch'in Dynasty.

HAN YÜ'S ATTACK ON TAOISM AND BUDDHISM

Han Yü (A.D. 786–824) was a famous literary figure of the T'ang Dynasty, a period that saw both Buddhism and Taoism rise to prominence. The imperial court was heavily influenced by these traditions, and, as a result, there was a broad sense that Confucianism shared points of view with Taoism and Buddhism, and that people in general were open to the combination of the "Three Traditions." Han Yü posed an exception to this general rule. He was committed to the Confucian tradition and the Confucian tradition alone. Though not a particularly powerful Confucian official, he used what influence he had to argue for the benefits brought to the state and the people by Confucian teachings. In making his point, he was highly critical of Taoism and Buddhism, both of which he believed were corrupting Chinese culture. In his own day he did not have any great success. However, later Confucians saw him as a major watershed figure in reviving Confucian cultural dominance.

In the spirit of a lone defender of Confucianism in a court heavily influenced by Taoist and Buddhist sympathies, Han Yü presented his most famous memorial to the throne. A Buddhist relic—an artifact that had supposedly belonged to the historical Buddha in India—had been presented to the emperor and was being kept at the court. Han Yü argued against displaying the relic, claiming that doing so was a violation of the teachings of the ancient Chinese sages. His arguments were very ethnocentric: He suggested that Buddhism was a religion of foreigners and had no place in China. He also declared that the teachings of the ancient sages were complete in themselves. From his point of view, the Five Classics and the ideas of the Confucians did not need to be supplemented by the teachings of others, particularly those from foreign religions. Han Yü claimed that Taoism and Buddhism, having rejected the Confucian teachings that provide a basis for the education of the individual and the ordering of society, had relinquished the right to serve as a foundation for peace and order. In his opinion, only Confucian teachings addressed the real issues of living in the world.

Though we most frequently describe China as "the Land of Three Religions" and imply by that designation a high level of toleration among the traditions as well as an understanding that an individual can participate in more than one tradition, this is not to say that people did not have preferences for a particular religious tradition. They did, at times, and those preferences might be strongly expressed. The spirit of Han Yü is clearly one of advocacy for Confucianism and a very critical stance toward other points of view. In this respect, he is not typical of most Confucians, but at the same time, he played an exceptionally important role in history. Han Yü became a model of advocacy for Confucianism that shaped the subsequent development of the Confucian tradition.

As Neo-Confucianism began to develop, its founders sought to establish the primacy of Confucian teachings as the starting point for all learning and education, and they saw the need to counter the influences of Taoism and Buddhism. Han Yü became a symbol of advocacy for basic Confucian teachings in the face of mounting opposition and seemingly insurmountable odds.

The spirit of Han Yü drove later Confucians to reassert the importance of what they saw as their own foundational teachings. This advocacy changed forever the landscape of Confucian discourse and the role that Neo-Confucians saw for themselves as advocates of the tradition. This development does not mean that there weren't largely cooperative relations among all three religions, but it does suggest that Confucians gave priority to their own foundation of teachings in their relations with other traditions.

MAY 4 MOVEMENT

The nineteenth century witnessed the slow demise of imperial China, the increasing influx of Western influence, and the agonizingly slow process of modernization. In the early twentieth century, China threw off the last vestiges of imperial rule with the revolution of 1911 and the establishment of the Republic of China. The next decades, however, brought Western involvement and several futile attempts to establish national stability and assert Chinese dominance. Modernization seemed to be going nowhere, and the populace, particularly the intellectuals, was increasingly frustrated with what was seen as a series of failures on China's part to address both its internal domestic issues and its relations with foreign powers. The May 4 Movement represents one of the most important displays of the Chinese intellectuals' and students' collective frustration with the internal modernization of China and the treatment of their nation by outsiders.

May 4, 1919, was a day of national protest during which large numbers of people spoke out against China's weakness in its dealings with foreign nations. The specific incident they were protesting was the handing over of German possessions in Shantung Province to Japan instead of China, as part of the Versailles peace settlement after World War I. The treatment China received suggested the degree to which it was seen by some nations as nothing more than a commodity to be parceled out as part of the spoils of war.

The May 4 Movement was named for this day of protest, but it also represented a broader effort that sought to bring about both modernization and increased power and dignity for China within the world community. As a broader movement, some scholars claim it may have originated as early as 1915 with the establishment of the revolutionary magazine *New Youth*, and it lasted until the late 1920s. Throughout this period, Chinese intellectuals and students argued vociferously in favor of modernization. The movement was driven by a high level of nationalist zeal to see a new and powerful China emerge.

The chief opponents of the May 4 Movement included anyone who wished to hold on to the old ways of Chinese culture. For the May 4 Movement, modernization was paramount and it had to be accomplished through the adoption of Western ways and the rejection of certain aspects of traditional Chinese culture. Specifically, the movement promoted what it saw as the benefits of Western science and democracy and the potential of these ideals to build a strong China. Traditional Chinese culture was seen as the cause of the weakness that had befallen China, both domestically and internationally.

The center of such traditional culture was, not surprisingly, perceived to be Confucianism. From this point of view, it was because of Confucianism that imperial rule had lasted so long. The Confucians were seen as supporters of the monarchy who did not want to accept the radical adoption of Western models for democracy and constitutional government. It was because of Confucianism that China's educational system was not modernized. Chinese society itself was seen as entrenched in old moral customs rather than based on the need to develop urban population centers and provide professional training. The Confucians were considered unresponsive to the idea of accommodating the changes that went along with the advent of the modern world.

With the growth of such attitudes, Confucianism was seen as virtually nothing but a symbol of the ancient ways. It was an easy target, and so the call for revolution became virtually synonymous with a call for the elimination of Confucianism. Such attacks created a crisis for the Confucian tradition in modern China. In fact, it was because of revolutionary movements and the general dismantling of any of the official roles traditionally assigned to the Confucians that a number of scholars concluded that Confucianism was effectively dead in the twentieth century.

CULTURAL REVOLUTION

Confucianism has never been in favor in the eyes of the Chinese Communist Party, and it is that party that established the People's Republic of China in 1949 and has ruled it ever since. Through the years of Communist rule, various criticisms have been made of the Confucian tradition and its founder. No period has been as critical, however, as the one that has come to be called the Cultural Revolution, short for the "Great Proletarian Cultural Revolution," or *wen wu ta-ko-ming*.

The Cultural Revolution was planned by China's leader Mao Tse-tung, along with his wife, Chiang Ch'ing, and several of her closest associates. Taking place between 1966 and 1976, it was born of the belief that Mao's revolutionary spirit was losing ground to a revival of traditional Chinese ways as well as the growth of governmental bureaucracy. It sought to cause sociopolitical upheaval throughout the country in order to reinstill the spirit of Communist revolution that had first brought the People's Republic of China into existence. Under the leadership of Mao and his designated officers, the Cultural Revolution commanded the loyalty of thousands of young people who became known as the Red Guards.

Red Guard members were directed to canvass the country to reestablish the ideals of the original Marxist revolution. In their zeal to carry out their mission, they relied on Mao as their source of inspiration, believing that all other sources were secondary, irrelevant, counterproductive, and, especially, counterrevolutionary. Members of the Red Guards carried the sayings of Mao with them everywhere in a volume that became known as the Little Red Book. The Red Guards believed that Mao's writings could provide guidance in any and all activities.

In the spirit of recapturing the revolution, the Red Guards rampaged across the countryside, destroying what could be seen as connected in any way to traditional Chinese culture. Traveling in China today, one can still see vestiges of the destruction brought by zealous members of the Red Guards, such as damage to historic sites. The Red Guards described their mission as rooting out the "Four Olds"—old culture, old ideas, old customs, and old habits. If there was one tradition that epitomized what the Red Guards considered the Four Olds, it was Confucianism. Already seen as counterrevolutionary, Confucianism was specifically targeted for attack by the Red Guards.

The assault on Confucianism took a number of forms. The Red Guards attacked and largely wrecked the temple at Confucius's birthplace of Ch'ü-fu, as well as his tomb and statues. Large numbers of Confucian writings were destroyed, as archives—seen as symbols of traditional ways—were ransacked. Prominent intellectuals whose thought seemed to reflect the Four Olds—particularly if they embraced Confucianism—were publicly ridiculed and forced to submit to self-criticism. The Red Guards also sought to undermine the traditional structure of the family, claiming that loyalty and special moral relations between family members must give way to fidelity to the state and an acceptance of the concept of class struggle. These latter ideas, rather than family ties, were to be the basis for all social relationships.

Eventually, those responsible for the Red Guards movement and the Cultural Revolution fell out of favor and became known as the Gang of Four. As the movement lost its power, there was an attempt to reinstate and reacknowledge the role of traditional Chinese culture, and with it, Confucianism. The Confucian Temple and Confucius's tomb were eventually restored.

Today, there is greater recognition in China of Confucianism, and toleration for the role played by traditional culture. No understanding of the general interpretation of Confucianism in the People's Republic of China is possible, however, without knowledge of the systematic attempt by the Cultural Revolution to rid China of all vestiges of its traditional ways.

As we have seen, even the Cultural Revolution did not eliminate Confucianism entirely, but it certainly did raise questions about how contemporary Confucianism may be defined or described. Anyone, even today, who would like to advocate Confucianism must be aware that a movement like the Cultural Revolution makes it far more challenging to present a Confucian agenda that fits within the contemporary world, and certainly within the People's Republic of China.

10

Confucianism in the World Today

*If you can practice these five things
with all the people, you can be called jen.
Courtesy, generosity, honesty,
persistence, and kindness . . .*

—Analects 17:6

H istorically, Confucianism has played a central role in the cultures of East and Southeast Asia. It permeated political and social elements of each of the cultures to which it was linked. It was essentially the Confucians who determined much of the character of each of the countries under Confucian influence. Confucianism touched the lives of all segments of the population, both the educated and uneducated.

With the advent of modernization within East and Southeast Asian cultures beginning in the nineteenth century, Confucianism's traditional role was challenged. Modernization essentially meant the introduction of Western culture. Because Western culture was very different from Asian custom, it was often difficult to implement. Though the various Asian cultures modernized in their own ways, there was one similarity among all of them. That common feature was a rejection, often radical in nature, of traditional worldviews in favor of embracing Western ideas. Although it is now recognized that Confucianism had been in large part responsible for the successful modernization of East and Southeast Asia, when the new wave of modernization began it was the first tradition to be thrown out. Confucianism represented everything that was wrong with the past, and it was viewed as a conservative force that was holding back Asian culture from becoming part of the modern world.

Because of this radical rejection of the ways of the past, Confucianism as a living tradition had been, by the beginning of the twentieth century, largely eradicated. Its role in government came to an end with the adoption of more radical and, in some cases, democratic structures. Its role in education ceased with the discontinuance of the civil service examination system. Education was now developed around Western models. Even the institutional traditions of the Confucian Temple died out as all ritual activity stopped.

CONTEMPORARY CHARACTER OF CONFUCIANISM

Was the Confucian tradition truly dead? Some observers believed that it had, in fact, been destroyed, and that it would play no future role in Asian cultures, let alone a role in the global context of late-twentieth-century ideas. Such reports of the tradition's demise, however, turned out to be premature and simply inaccurate. Old ideas and practices do not die easily. Those who argued that Confucianism was dead did not take into account the fact that Confucianism was a deep-seated tradition that had formed a central part of the cultures in which it had played a role. Doing away with the formal institutions that had supported Confucianism took the tradition out of the limelight, but did not completely eliminate it. Although Confucianism was, at best, unpopular to discuss, people in many cases tended to behave in the same way they always had. In other words, getting rid of Confucianism as a formal institution did not stop its influence across the broad sweep of Asian culture as a deeply imbedded set of practices and attitudes. As a result, Confucianism today still plays a very important role. It has never regained its prominent place in major institutions, and in many ways it is not even formally recognized. Still, its ideas and rituals remain powerfully diffused throughout Asian cultures.

CONFUCIAN IDEAS IN MODERN PRACTICE

There are two main ways in which contemporary Confucianism may be discussed. The first is to identify Confucianism with a set of ideas and practices that are thoroughly integrated into the cultures of East and Southeast Asia. In this view, aspects of Confucianism are simply part of the culture. They may not necessarily even be viewed as Confucian by the tradition's participants. In fact, in most cases, someone might be quite surprised to learn that the origin of an idea he or she supports was actually Confucian.

A number of characteristics of contemporary East and Southeast Asian societies reflect Confucian tradition. These are cultures that value the creation of a moral society. One way in which such values are propagated is through the moral relationships between individuals and across populations. Underlying these behaviors is the fundamentally Confucian premise that humans should act in moral ways toward others. Filial piety, the proper relation of parents and children, may seem old-fashioned, yet Confucian-influenced Asian cultures remain heavily affected by such fundamental norms of behavior. One is likely to hear, even from Asians who have no knowledge of Confucianism per se, that filial piety is the foundation for the order of society itself.

Another fundamental value in East and Southeast Asian cultures is the emphasis placed on education. Though the traditional Confucian curriculum has been done away with, and the civil service examination system is now only a footnote in history, the importance attributed to a solid education is a fundamentally Confucian belief. The focus of learning in modern Asian cultures remains associated with the concept that people can transform themselves, their society, and ultimately the world for the better through a proper education.

THE NEW CONFUCIANISM

The second way to describe the contemporary Confucian tradition is in terms of what might be described as the "New Confucianism." This movement is led by a group of prominent thinkers who view the Confucian tradition in part as a set of viable ideas and practices for the present generation and for generations yet to come. These individuals are self-consciously Confucian, even in an age where Confucianism as a formal practice has, for all intents and purposes, ceased to exist.

Included among the New Confucians are prominent thinkers such as Fung Yu-lan (1895–1990), T'ang Chün-I (1909–1978), and Mou Tsung-san (1909–1994) in China, and the contemporary Confucians Okada Takehiko in Japan and Tu Wei-ming in the United States. The life work of Fung, T'ang, and Mou was to formulate a system of thought that took into account the richness of Western ideas, but remained fundamentally Confucian in orientation. These individuals were essentially modern-day Confucian philosophers who, during their lifetimes, molded elements of Confucian thought to fit into the world of contemporary philosophy. Okada and Tu are two Confucians who are still making significant contributions to the ongoing evolution of contemporary Confucianism.

Okada Takehiko

In the mid-1970s, as a young scholar, I was given the opportunity to study in Kyoto, Japan, for a year. Before I left the United States, I was told that, if at all possible, I should try to meet Okada Takehiko, the famous Confucian scholar. He lived nowhere near Kyoto, but in Fukuoka, far to the south on Japan's major southern island Kyushu. For this reason alone, I did not anticipate that I would be able to meet him. It turned out, however, that I did have an opportunity to meet Okada during my year abroad. I traveled to Fukuoka to consult with him on a translation I was doing of one of his books into English. I had assumed that Professor Okada would be a scholar of Confucianism, but what I found was someone who was first and foremost a Confucian scholar. The difference is critical!

Okada met me at the train station, and during the taxi ride to his home, he turned to me and said, "I feel that the world is in tremendous moral and spiritual decline. What do you think can be done about it?" This question was not one that would be posed by someone who simply studies Confucianism. Okada was not asking me what my Western historical tradition had to say on the question, or even what I, a particular thinker from that tradition, believed. He was asking me directly, with no intermediary of text or regard to any particular tradition. It was the "teacher" Okada saying to the "scholar" Rodney Taylor, "Our world is in decline. How do we meet the challenge?" The person I had just met was the living embodiment of the Confucian tradition. Confucianism was no longer a historical tradition of texts and thinkers—it was standing in front of me!

As it turned out, I have since made many trips to Fukuoka to visit with Okada. I have spent time engaging him in formal interviews about Confucianism, its past, present, and future. Clearly, Okada sees a place for Confucianism in the modern world. In fact, from his point of view, Confucianism is not only suited to various Asian cultures, but to the larger world in general. Confucianism is, in his mind, a global teaching. This is not to say that all of the history of the tradition, its schools, divisions, and its countless major thinkers, will ever be of much interest to the general population in Asia, much less the world at large. Rather, Okada suggests that out of the rich heritage of Confucian tradition has come a set of ideas and practices that are relevant both to our age and future ages. In fact, he believes these ideas might be uniquely suited to addressing contemporary issues.

What Okada sees as Confucianism's unique contribution to the modern world of thought revolves around his own sense of the essential Confucian teachings. It is a contribution of broad-based values, beginning with the principle of the goodness of human nature. Okada believes that if humanity builds upon a belief in the goodness of human nature, then we will treat ourselves and others in moral ways and, as a result, the world will be transformed to a moral state. He refers to Mencius's idea that no human by nature can bear to see the suffering of another. This point of view might be somewhat shaken by the undeniable reality that the world is full of cruelty and violence, but it rests in the belief that we must always begin with the premise that humankind is naturally good.

Okada believes that the modern world is dominated by science and technology, and that the essential moral nature of humankind plays little role. He calls for the reinvention of human moral value and its exercise in all aspects of our contemporary world. He says that only when science and technology are governed by moral order and purposes will the world truly experience progress.

What does Okada say about the future of Confucianism itself?

OKADA TAKEHIKO ON SCIENCE

Okada Takehiko is considered one of a very small number of Confucians still living in Japan today. He is both a very famous Confucian scholar with a distinguished record of scholarship in Chinese and Japanese Neo-Confucianism, as well as a living Confucian. His thought represents a Confucian response to many of the major changes and developments in the world that we are now a part of and that we often take for granted. Seldom do we have the opportunity to have a Confucian perspective on various elements of this world. The following is an excerpt from a discussion with Okada about science and its dominance in our world today. In it, Okada expresses both his admiration for science as well as his concerns for the way in which it has developed. His interpretation is based on the Confucian sense of *jen*, or "humaneness." He believes that all human action must be based in moral respect for other human beings and ultimately for all life itself.

> I have a concern about the way in which science has developed. Its development has reached a point were it threatens the very existence of human life. The development of science should be for the benefit of the human community, but if there is a threat posed, then we need to be duly concerned about such developments. Nevertheless, we can't stop science and its developments, for much of science is necessary for the human community. If we are going to make science totally responsive to the needs of the human community, we must let everyone— scientists and non-scientists alike—learn the importance of human life. In speaking of the importance of human life, it is essential to realize the importance of one's own life as well as the lives of others. We live in the same world together and mutual respect for life is a prerequisite. From my point of view Confucianism provides a suitable basis for this perspective. At the center of this perspective lies the Confucian idea of being in community with others. In short, one can live only by living in the company of others. In order to do this it is essential to follow the rules of society. The basis of Confucian ethics is to have consideration for the other person's heart. If we extend this concept, we can include all of nature.*

* Rodney L. Taylor, *The Confucian Way of Contemplation: Okada Takehiko and the Tradition of Quiet-Sitting*, Columbia, SC: University of South Carolina Press, 1988, p. 199.

He told me that it was difficult to discuss the future of Confucianism because it was still associated with the old-fashioned ideas that had held Japan back from modernization. However, he added, the name itself, Confucianism, was no longer important either to him or for the future of the tradition's ideas and practices. He imagined that, in the future, it would make no difference whether something called Confucianism existed or not. What he was concerned about was the continuation of what he saw as the fundamental teachings of Confucianism, regardless of how they might be labeled. In his mind, these teachings focus primarily on respect for life. He said to me, "We don't really need to have Confucianism as Confucianism in the future. All we need is the respect for human life and human dignity."

Tu Wei-ming

Tu Wei-ming, whose views are in some ways similar to those of Okada Takehiko, sees a role for Confucianism not only within the context of contemporary society, but for future generations as well. He also sees the Confucian tradition as reaching beyond its roots in various Asian cultures and becoming part of a global dialogue about critical issues. Confucianism is anything but the virtually dead tradition it was at the start of the twentieth century. In fact, for Tu Wei-ming, the advent of the twenty-first century has injected new life and vitality into Confucianism as a global perspective, giving it perhaps more potential to affect the entire world than it has had at any time in its long and illustrious history.

What does Tu Wei-ming believe is at the center of this new springing to life for the Confucian tradition? To understand the scholar's answer, we must first know something about the background and approach of Tu Wei-ming himself. Like Okada, Tu is a highly trained scholar of Confucianism. In fact, he was a student of one of the great thinkers of modern China, Mou Tsung-san, who was himself associated with the New Confucianism. As his career developed, Tu Wei-ming was principally known as a Chinese historian, highly trained in Confucian and general Chinese intellectual traditions, but equally fluent in Western philosophy. As he studied Confucianism, Tu appears to have begun to see that there was more to the subject than a simple historical reconstruction of the tradition's ideas. He found value not only in Confucianism's past, but in its capacity to be adapted for use in the present and even into the future. As he developed this line of thought, Tu transformed from a scholar of Confucianism to a Confucian scholar.

Tu has more and more been recognized as a major Confucian scholar of the modern generation. In addition to conducting major research in the history of the ideas of Confucianism, Tu has created what has been referred to as a new Confucian commentary tradition. The commentary is on a Confucian classic, the *Chung yung*, or Doctrine of the Mean, and it presents the text from within the tradition. At the political level, Tu was invited to assist the government of Singapore in matters of education and ethics. In this role, he become a Confucian advisor to the government, playing a role not unlike the traditional one that Confucians often took on in East and Southeast Asian countries during premodern times.

Tu's agenda is now focused on larger issues at the global level. He believes that if Confucianism does survive, it is now approaching what he calls its "Third Epoch." In its first phases, it remained Asia-centered. If it is to be taken seriously at the global level, however, then its agenda must be a global one. When asked if such a change is possible, Tu says yes. Confucianism has a great deal to say about global issues and it is in doing so that the future of the tradition lies. Tu sees the basic moral teachings of Confucianism as fundamental to any future discussion of human rights. He sees the Confucian stress on the education of the individual as key to an understanding of human freedom. He also believes that the Confucian vision of a shared moral universe in which all living things are one is basic to any conversation about the future relation of humankind to the environment.

In the minds of thinkers such as Okada Takehiko and Tu Wei-ming, Confucianism still has a major role to play in the contemporary—and future—political, cultural, and social world. The Confucian tradition, therefore, is an important one, not only to the cultures that have embraced it in the past, but to those cultures to which it is still largely unknown. So long as it is capable of adjusting and adapting to address new global concerns and issues, it has the potential to be a critical influence in all discussions on the future of our planet Earth.

(Chronology refers to Chinese history unless otherwise stated.)

Antiquity—Third millennium B.C.

2852   Fu Hsi—Culture Hero

2737   Shen Hung—Culture Hero

2697   Yellow Emperor—Culture Hero

2357   Yao—Sage ruler

2255   Shun—Sage ruler

2205   Yü—Sage ruler

1766–1122 Shang Dynasty—First historic dynasty

1100 B.C.
Chou Dynasty
is founded

770
Spring and
Autumn
Period begins

202
Han Dynasty—
the official state
establishment of
Confucianism begins

371
Mencius
is born
(dies 289)

A.D. 619
Confucian Temple built in capital

A.D. 630
Confucian Temples built in
all provinces

A.D. 960
Sung Dynasty begins

| 1100 | 700 | 500 | 200 BC | AD | 1000 |

551
Confucius is born
(dies 479)

480
Warring States Period begins; the
"Hundred Schools of Thought,"
including Confucianism,
Taoism, and Legalism, grow

212
Burying of the Scholars

213
Burning of the Books

214
Construction of the Great Wall completed

221
Ch'in Dynasty is founded

1122–221 Chou Dynasty

Twelfth century—Founding of Chou Dynasty, which
shows a very high level of Confucian interst
King Wen—founder
King Wu—founder
King Cheng—founder
Duke of Chou—regent for King Cheng

722–481 Spring and Autumn Period

551–479 Confucius—founder of Confucian tradition

480–221 Warring States Period

371–289 Mencius—formulator of Confucian teaching

1911
Republican period begins;
Republic proclaimed

1919
May 4 Movement
takes place

1905
Civil service examination
is abolished

1949
Nationalist China is defeated
by Communists; establishment
of Communist China and
movement of Nationalist
China to Taiwan

1900
Boxer Rebellion takes place,
in which China revolts
against foreign dominance

1200   **1900**   **2000**

1894–1895
Sino-Japanese War causes
destruction in China

1956
"Hundred Flowers"
speech by Mao Tse-tung

1644
Ch'ing Dynasty begins

1368
Ming Dynasty is founded

1966
Cultural Revolution, which
attempts to eliminate the
influence of traditional ideas
(including Confucianism),
begins (movement ends in 1976)

1279
Yüan Dynasty begins

CHRONOLOGY

298–230	Hsün Tzu—formulator of Confucian teaching

221–207 Ch'in Dynasty (which opposes Conficianism)

213	Burning of the Books
212	Burying of the Scholars

206 B.C.–A.D. 220
Han Dynasty—Official state establishment of Confucianism

195 B.C.	Sacrifice offered to Confucius
141–87 B.C.	Emperor Han Wu-ti; Chinese expansion to Korea and Vietnam
136 B.C.	Appointments of Scholars of Five Classics
124 B.C.	Civil service examination inaugurated
A.D. 175	Five Classics and Analects engraved in stone

Third century–918
Korea—Three Kingdoms and Silla periods

	Third Century—Confucianism in Korea
682	Establishment of Royal Confucian Academy
788	Establishment of state examination system

A.D. 573–621
Japan—Shotoku Taishi and Confucianism

604	17 Article Constitution
645	Taika Reform

618–907 T'ang Dynasty—Dominance of Buddhism

619	Confucian Temple built in capital
630	Confucian Temples built in all provinces
768–824	Han Yü—reviver of Confucianism
843–845	Persecution of Buddhism

918–1392 Korea—Koryo Kingdom

1243–1306 An Hyang—Introduction of Neo-Confucianism

1367 Royal Confucian Academy rebuilt

960–1279 Sung Dynasty—Growth of Neo-Confucianism

960–1127 Northern Sung period

1127–1279 Southern Sung period

1017–1073 Chou Tun-i—Neo-Confucian

1020–1077 Chang Tsai—Neo-Confucian

1033–1107 Ch'eng I—Neo-Confucian

1130–1200 Chu Hsi—Neo-Confucian

1279–1368 Yüan Dynasty—China under Mongol rule

1392–1910 Korea—Chosen Dynasty

1501–1570 Yi T'oegye—Neo-Confucian

1894 Civil service examination suspended

1368–1644 Ming Dynasty—School of Mind grows

1472–1529 Wang Yang-ming—Neo-Confucian

1603–1868 Japan—Tokugawa Period

1561–1619 Fujiwara Seika—Neo-Confucian

1583–1657 Hayashi Razan—Neo-Confucian

1618–1682 Yamazaki Ansai—Neo-Confucian

1630–1714 Kaibara Ekken—Neo-Confucian

1608–1648 Nakae Toju—Neo-Confucian

1868 Beginning of Meiji Period

1644–1912 Ch'ing Dynasty—Last imperial dynasty

1851–1868 Taiping Rebellion

CHRONOLOGY

1894–1895	Sino-Japanese War
1895–1990	Fung Yu-lan—New Confucian
1898	Chinese concessions to Western powers
1900	Boxer Rebellion
1905	Civil service examination abolished
1909–1978	T'ang Chün-I—New Confucian
1909–1994	Mou Tsung-san—New Confucian
1912–1949	**Republican period**
1912	End of dynastic history–Republic proclaimed
1919	May 4 Movement—anti-Confucian
1949	Nationalist China defeated by Communists
1949–present	**People's Republic of China and Nationalist China**
1949	Establishment of Communist China
1956	"Hundred Flowers" speech by Mao Tse-tung
1966–1976	Cultural Revolution—anti-Confucian

Berthrong, John H. *Transformations of the Confucian Way.* Westview Press, 1998.

Birrell, Anne. *Chinese Mythology: An Introduction.* Johns Hopkins University Press, 1993.

Chan, Wing-tsit. *A Source Book in Chinese Philosophy.* Princeton University Press, 1963.

Ching, Julia. *The Religious Thought of Chu Hsi.* Oxford University Press, 2000.

Ch'oe, Yongho, Peter H. Lee, and William Theodore De Bary, eds. *Sources of Korean Tradition,* Vol. 2. Columbia University Press, 2000.

De Bary, William Theodore, and John W. Chaffee, eds. *Neo-Confucian in Education: The Formative Stage.* University of California Press, 1989.

De Bary, William Theodore, and Irene Bloom, eds. *Sources of Chinese Tradition,* 2nd ed., Vol. 1. Columbia University Press, 1999.

Gardner, Daniel K., trans. *Learning to Be a Sage: Selections from the Conversations of Master Chu, Arranged Topically.* University of California Press, 1990.

Fingarette, Herbert. *Confucius: The Secular as Sacred.* Harper & Row, 1972.

Hall, David L., and Roger Ames. *Thinking Through Confucius.* State University of New York Press, 1987.

Kalton, Michael C. *To Become a Sage: The Ten Diagrams on Sage Leaning by Yi T'oegye.* Columbia University Press, 1988.

Lau, D.C., trans. *Confucius: The Analects (Lun-yü).* Penguin Books Ltd., 1979.

———. *Mencius.* Penguin Books Ltd., 1970.

BIBLIOGRAPHY

Lee, Peter H., and William Theodore De Bary, eds. *Sources of Korean Tradition,* Vol. 1. Columbia University Press, 1997.

Overmyer, Daniel L. *Religions of China: The World as a Living System.* Harper & Row, 1986.

Paper, Jordan, and Laurence G. Thompson. *The Chinese Way in Religion,* 2nd ed. Wadsworth, 1998.

Schwartz, Benjamin I. *The World of Thought in Ancient China.* The Belknap Press of Harvard University Press, 1985.

Shryock, John K. *The Origin and Development of the State Cult of Confucius.* Paragon Book Reprint Corporation, 1966.

Taylor, Rodney L. *The Confucian Way of Contemplation: Okada Takehiko and the Tradition of Quiet-Sitting.* University of South Carolina Press, 1988.

———. *The Illustrated Encyclopedia of Confucianism,* Vol. 2. The Rosen Publishing Group, 2004.

———. *An Introduction to the Confucian Religious Life.* E.J. Brill, 1986.

———. *The Religious Dimensions of Confucianism.* State University of New York Press, 1990.

Thompson, Laurence G. *Chinese Religion: An Introduction,* 5th ed. Wadsworth, 1998.

Tsunoda, Ryusaku, William Theodore De Bary, and Donald Keene, eds. *Sources of Japanese Tradition,* Vols. 1 & 2. Columbia University Press, 1964.

Tucker, Mary Evelyn. *Moral and Spiritual Cultivation in Japanese Neo-Confucianism: The Life and Thought of Kaibara Ekken (1630–1714).* State University of New York Press, 1989.

Tu, Wei-ming. *Centrality and Commonality: An Essay on Confucian Religiousness.* State University of New York Press, 1989.

Waley, Arthur. *The Analects of Confucius*. George Allen & Unwin, 1938.

———. *The Book of Songs*. Houghton Mifflin, 1937.

Watson, Burton, trans. *Hsün Tzu: Basic Writings*. Columbia University Press, 1963.

Wilson, Thomas A., ed. *On Sacred Grounds: Culture, Society , Politics and the Formation of the Cult of Confucius*, Harvard East Asian Monographs 217. Harvard University Asia Center, 2002.

Yao, Xinzhong. *An Introduction to Confucianism*. Cambridge University Press, 2000.

FURTHER READING

PRIMARY SOURCES

Chan, Wing-tsit. *A Source Book in Chinese Philosophy.* Princeton University Press, 1963.

Ch'oe, Yongho, Peter H. Lee, and WilliamTheodore De Bary, eds. *Sources of Korean Tradition,* Vol. 2. Columbia University Press, 2000.

De Bary, William Theodore, and Irene Bloom, eds. *Sources of Chinese Tradition,* 2nd ed., Vol. 1. Columbia University Press, 1999.

Gardner, Daniel K., trans. *Learning to Be a Sage: Selections from the Conversations of Master Chu, Arranged Topically.* University of California Press, 1990.

Lau, D.C., trans. *Confucius: The Analects (Lun-yü).* Penguin Books Ltd., 1979.

————. *Mencius.* Middlesex: Penguin Books Ltd., 1970.

Tsunoda, Ryusaku, William Theodore De Bary, and Donald Keene, eds. *Sources of Japanese Tradition,* Vols. 1 & 2. Columbia University Press, 1964.

SECONDARY SOURCES

Berthrong, John H. *Transformations of the Confucian Way.* Westview Press, 1998.

Fingarette, Herbert. *Confucius: The Secular as Sacred.* Harper & Row, 1972.

Hall, David L., and Roger Ames. *Thinking Through Confucius.* State University of New York Press, 1987.

Paper, Jordan, and Laurence G. Thompson. *The Chinese Way in Religion,* 2nd ed. Wadsworth, 1998.

Taylor, Rodney L. *The Confucian Way of Contemplation: Okada Takehiko and the Tradition of Quiet-Sitting.* University of South Carolina Press, 1988.

————. *The Illustrated Encyclopedia of Confucianism*, 2 vols. The Rosen Publishing Group, 2004.

————. *An Introduction to the Confucian Religious Life*. E.J. Brill, 1986.

————. *The Religious Dimensions of Confucianism*. State University of New York Press, 1990.

Yao, Xinzhong. *An Introduction to Confucianism*. Cambridge University Press, 2000.

WEBSITES

China, Confucianism, and Philosophies
http://www.index-china.com/index-english/
Confucius%20and%20Confucianism.html
Presents views on Confucianism as it relates to Chinese history and current affairs.

Chinese Literature, Philosophy and Religion
http://www.chinaknowledge.de/Literature/Classics/confucius.htm
Contains information about the teachings of Confucianism, the life of Confucius, and general Chinese history.

Chinese Philosophy Page
http://main.chinesephilosophy.net/rujia.html
Contains translations of many Confucian sources as well as links to related websites.

Confucianism
http://www.sacred-texts.com/cfu/
Contains translated versions of key Confucian scriptures, including the Five Classics and Four Books.

Confucianism: A Bibliography
http://www.anu.edu.au/asianstudies/publications/confbib.htm
This site, maintained by the Australian National University, contains extensive information on the Confucian tradition, including essays by well-known scholars.

FURTHER READING

Confucianism and Taoism Digital Texts Resources
http://www.human.toyogakuen-u.ac.jp/~acmuller/contaolink.htm
Contains writings from Confucianism and other Asian religious traditions.

Confucianism in Korea
http://www.asianinfo.org/asianinfo/korea/rel/confucianism.htm
Provides information about the history of Confucianism in Korea.

The Harmony Project
http://www.theharmonyproject.org/sacredpaths/confucianism/
Provides excerpts of Confucian literature and comparative information that relates Confucianism to other world religions.

The Interfaith Center of New York
http://www.interfaithcenter.org/confucianism.shtml
Discusses the background of Confucianism and provides information about Confucianism in the United States.

INDEX

INDEX

Shih chi ("Records of the Historian"), 111, 112
Shih ching (Classic or Book of Poetry), 19, 34, 35-36, 88-89, 110
shih hsüeh (School of Practical Learning), 14-15, 58
shih-tien ceremony (Twice Yearly Confucian Ceremony), 61, 63, 65, 66, 68-70
Shinto, 4, 8, 85
shu (sympathy), 48
Shu ching (Classic or Book of History), 34, 35, 110
Shun, 33
Six Arts, 86, 93
Six Classics, 31.
  See also Five Classics
Sixth Classic (Classic of Music), 34, 38, 93
social ethics, and Confucianism, 5-6, 28-29, 105
social reinforcement of Confucian values, 96-105
  and education of children, 100-103
  and holidays, 97-99
  and life passage rituals, 99-100
  and social ethics, 105.
  See also Confucian Temple; family
"Son of Heaven". *See T'ien-tzu*
Southeast Asia, 4, 8, 16, 85, 97, 121, 122, 128
Spring and Autumn Period, 19
steles, 66
Sung, state of, 21
Sung Dynasty, 13, 14, 16, 31, 39, 100, 101, 103, 107
supernatural elements, 23, 29, 71
sympathy. *See shu*

Ta-ch'eng chih-sheng K'ung-Tzu hsien-shih ("Teacher of Antiquity, Confucius, of Greatest Accomplishment and Highest Sageliness"), 68

ta-ch'eng tien (Hall of Great Accomplishments), 65, 66
Ta hsüeh (Great Learning), 8, 39, 40, 74, 76, 105
t'ai-lao (Great Offering), 62-63, 68, 71
T'ai Tsung, 62
T'ang Chün-I, 123-124
T'ang Dynasty, 12, 39, 56, 62, 113-114
Taoism, 4, 5, 13, 14, 20, 33-34, 55, 56, 58, 85, 87, 91, 92, 100, 113-114
Teacher's Day, 98
technology, and Okada, 125
Temple of Confucius. *See K'ung tzu miao*
Temple of Culture. *See wen miao*
Temple of the Comprehensive King. *See Wen hsüan wang miao*
Temple of the Sage of Antiquity. *See hsien sheng miao*
Third Epoch, 128
"Three Character Classic". *See San Tzu Ching*
Three Obediences and Four Virtues. *See san-ts'ung ssu-te*
Three Traditions, 113
T'ien (Heaven), 6-7, 10, 22, 25-26, 27, 29, 30, 34, 35, 36, 38, 40, 42, 45, 51, 71, 73, 74, 93
T'ien ming ("Mandate of Heaven"), 45, 74
T'ien-tzu ("Son of Heaven"), 11, 45, 53, 74
Tokugawa Period, 16
tsu miao (ancestral shrine), 82-83, 97
Tu Wei-ming, 123, 124, 127-129
Twice Yearly Confucian Ceremony. *See shih-tien* ceremony

unicorn, and Confucian Temple, 67
utility. *See yung*

values. *See* social reinforcement of Confucian values

PICTURE CREDITS

RODNEY L. TAYLOR is professor of Religious Studies at the University of Colorado at Boulder, where he has been on the faculty since 1978. His degrees include a B.A. (1966) from the University of Southern California, an M.A. (1968) from the University of Washington, and a Ph.D. (1974) from Columbia University. In addition to holding a faculty position, he has served in a variety of administrative positions on the campus, including Director of Asian Studies, Chairman of the Department of Religious Studies, Associate Dean of the Graduate School, Interim Dean of the Graduate School, and Associate Vice Chancellor for Graduate Education. His books include *The Cultivation of Sagehood as a Religious Goal in Neo-Confucianism: A Study of Selected Writings of Kao P'an-lung, 1562–1626* (1978) (with F. M. Denny), *The Holy Book in Comparative Perspective* (1985), *The Way of Heaven: An Introduction to the Confucian Religious Life* (1986), *The Confucian Way of Contemplation: Okada Takehiko and the Tradition of Quiet-Sitting* (1988) (with J. Watson), *They Shall Not Hurt: Human Suffering and Human Caring* (1989), *The Religious Dimensions of Confucianism* (1990), and *The Illustrated Encyclopedia of Confucianism* (2004).

MARTIN E. MARTY, an ordained minister in the Evangelical Lutheran Church in America, is the Fairfax M. Cone Distinguished Service Professor Emeritus at the University of Chicago Divinity School, where he taught for thirty-five years. Marty has served as president of the American Academy of Religion, the American Society of Church History, and the American Catholic Historical Association, and was also a member of two U.S. presidential commissions. He is currently Senior Regent at St. Olaf College in Northfield, Minnesota. Marty has written more than fifty books, including the three-volume *Modern American Religion* (University of Chicago Press). His book *Righteous Empire* was a recipient of the National Book Award.